Judaism from Above the Clouds

A Handbook for the Wondering Jew

ISBN:1482364980
ISBN-13: 9781482364989

DEDICATION

This book is dedicated to my beloved wife Fraida Sara, and our children, Raphael Yitzchak Ephraim OBM, Chaya Feiga Reizl, ElieMelech Chaim, Sholom DovBer, Kaila Rochel, Nechama Rivka, and Yisroel Zvi Hirsh, *Sheyichu*.

Our sages state, "The beginning is wedged in the end." This book is dedicated to the Rebbe, M.M. Schneerson, MHM.

According to the Zohar, "When the *Tzadik* departs, he is to be found in all the worlds even more than in his lifetime." In other words, the Rebbe continues to guide Jews throughout the world with boundless love and affection. May this work help to immediately reveal Isaiah's prophecy (Isaiah 11:9) of a time "when the world will be filled with the knowledge of G-d as water covers the sea."

What Readers Have to Say

"Judaism from Above the Clouds provides a comprehensive overview of all aspects of Judaism. It is impressive that a topic so vast could be covered so thoroughly in such a concise manner. No longer must any Jew be intimidated by Torah-true Judaism. Instead, in a short period of time, he can be empowered to delve into greater observance. This is a great reference book to begin an exploration into all areas of Judaism."

Michael L. Moritz, M.D., Associate Professor, Pediatrics; Medical Director, Pediatric Dialysis, Children's Hospital of Pittsburgh, University of Pittsburgh Medical Center (UPMC), Pittsburgh, PA

"The biggest challenge for any introductory text to Judaism is answering "why" not "what." In Judaism from Above the Clouds, Leibel Estrin grounds virtually every ritual observance in the wealth of *Chassidic* philosophy that explains why each tradition is important and how they fit together. For that reason, it's worthwhile for any Jew who wants to open the door into his or her faith."

Eric Lidji, writer, columnist, Pittsburgh, PA

"Judaism from Above the Clouds is tailor-made for people who are interested in Judaism and want to know the lay of the land. It is the ideal stepping stone for those who want to go further." **Dovid Sears, New York, author of Compassion for Humanity in the Jewish Tradition, The Vision of Eden; Animal Welfare and Vegetarianism in Jewish Law and others.**

"*Judaism from Above the Clouds* gives brief synopses on a wide range of Jewish topics and still provides a great amount of depth. The author has a way of expressing complicated insights in such a clear and concise manner that people with diverse backgrounds and varying levels of knowledge can pick up this book and gain new understandings from it." **Leiba Herman, Chatham University, Class of 2013, Pittsburgh, PA**

ACKNOWLEDGMENTS

I would like to thank the *Mashpia* (spiritual advisor) of Pittsburgh's Chabad community, HaRav Yisroel Meir ben Reb Zvi Hirsh Altein, OBM, who carefully reviewed this manuscript. His patience and his perception were truly remarkable. I also thank my *mechutan*, Rabbi Yehezkel Lebovic, and Rabbi Aaron Herman for their astute and helpful comments.

According to communications theorist Marshal McLuhan, "the medium is the message." From this perspective, *Judaism from Above the Clouds* owes much of its clarity to Nick Pascuzzi's graphic design. His talent is only exceeded by his patience.

How to Approach this Book

Most books are read from the beginning through to the end. You can approach *Judaism from Above the Clouds* that way or you can skip around, reading sections that interest you. Just take time to think about what you've read and if you have a question about how Jewish law applies to your particular situation, ask your local Orthodox rabbi. If you want to send general comments, questions, compliments or (gulp) criticisms, please email len.estrin@gmail.com.

Introduction: What Drives Man's Behavior?

It's a question that theologians, philosophers, scientists, and psychologists have been trying to answer for centuries. About 70 years ago, an Austrian psychiatrist Viktor Frankl came up with an explanation, and perhaps, one answer. In Frankl's view, man is driven by the search for meaning.

Frankl believed that, to previous generations, the responsibilities associated with family, community, etc. provided that meaning. However technological change and social/political systems have addressed most of the immediate needs facing family and community, leaving us to once again search for meaning in our lives. Frankl theorized that the inability to find meaning leads to addiction, aggression or depression.

What can bring meaning to man? Wealth? Fame? Success? Often, these are transitory, leaving those who tied their self-worth to them living in the past. Yet there is something that can provide meaning to man under all circumstances and all phases of one's life. It is the Torah (also known as the Five Books of Moses).

The Torah represents Divine Wisdom. Eternal and endless, it is a wellspring of knowledge, as relevant today as it was 3,000 years ago. Furthermore, the Torah is unique in that it helps us to live our lives in the most fulfilling manner possible now, while preparing us for the journey that follows once our life ends.

The question can be asked, "If the Torah has so much to offer, why do few people observe it?" Before we answer, let's look at its source. Most of us grew up in an assimilated society that promoted pleasure as a goal, not a byproduct, of a life well-lived. Over time, the values and worldview of that society became ours. So now many of us look at Judaism and Torah through the unrealistic prism of movies, television, and the Internet.

There is another problem. For many of us, our "formal" Jewish education ended with our bar or bas mitzvah. The result has been disastrous. We judge Judaism using the intellectual equivalent of a grade-school education. Along with our own ignorance, the ignorance spread by popular culture, contributes to the problem.

Therefore, if relatively few people observe the Torah, it's because so many don't understand it. This book attempts to address the situation. It outlines Jewish ideas and ideals from many perspectives but with one goal: to provide information you can use to make knowledgeable decisions as a thinking Jew.

An I for an I; not an "eye for an eye."

Perhaps the most misquoted verse in scripture is, "But if there be a fatality, then you shall award a life for life; an eye for an eye, a tooth for a tooth, a hand for a hand, a foot for a foot; a burn for a burn, a wound for a wound, a bruise for a bruise." (*Shemos* 21:24) According to secular understanding, the verse implies that one who injures another should be punished by receiving the same injury. However, the same injury will affect different people in different ways. So it's impossible to fulfill the *mitzvah* of "an eye for an eye" literally.

The Torah must be referring to something else. How do we know? The Hebrew term is *eyian tachas eyian. Tachas* means "in place of." Elsewhere in the Torah, the *tachas* refers to monetary compensation. So the Rabbis knew that it must mean monetary compensation here, as well.

If the Torah wanted us to compensate someone with money, why didn't it say so? The answer: we could easily miss the point. Compensating someone for the damage we caused could become as ordinary as buying milk. Therefore, the Torah stresses that we should feel another person's pain as if it were our own.

1. The Creator

The core of Judaism, and of all existence, is G-d. Nothing exists outside of G-d. Maimonides[1], the great Jewish philosopher, physician, and scholar, opens his compendium of Jewish law, the *Mishneh Torah* with, "The foundation of foundations and the pillar of wisdom is to know that there is a Primary Being who brought into being all existence. All the beings of the heavens, the earth, and what is between them came into existence, only from the truth of His being."[2] Maimonides is indicating several things:

There is only one Prime Force in the universe.

G-d existed before creation and will continue to exist forever. He is both eternal and unchanging. Anything, and everything, whether it's the stars, the forces of nature, good and evil, mankind, and all of existence derive from G-d. In essence, nothing exists independently from G-d. The apparent

---

[1] Rabbi Moshe ben Maimon (1135 CE – 1204 BCE). Also known as the Rambam. The Rambam authored *The Book of Commandments, Guide for the Perplexed,* and his comprehensive codification of Jewish Law, the *Mishneh Torah.*
[2] Maimonides, *Mishneh Torah, Hilchos Yesodei HaTorah,* translated by Rabbi Eliyahu Touger, Moznaim Publishing Corp., New York, 1989, P. 138

independence of reality is only from our perspective as created beings. In truth, G-d is the ultimate reality.

Second, G-d is not physical, yet is perfect in every manner.

Maimonides states, "G-d is one. He is neither two nor more than two, but one. The oneness of any of the individual things that exist in the universe is unlike His unity."[3] In short, G-d's unity is both unique and indivisible. This also means that G-d has no shape, form, or matter. G-d is above and beyond anything that we can conceive. Again, we return to Maimonides, "He is the Knower. He is the Subject of Knowledge, and He is the Knowledge itself. All is One."[4]

Third, G-d is the vitalizing Force of existence.

Some philosophies state that G-d created the world and monitors it from afar, allowing the cosmos to run on its own, similar to a watchmaker who installs a battery and intercedes only when necessary.

Judaism rejects this concept. Although G-d's presence is hidden from our mortal eyes, G-d continually sustains creation. If G-d withdrew His sustaining force even for the tiniest fraction of a second, the world would cease to exist; not only that, it would be as if the world never existed at all. (For a deeper explanation of the way Infinite G-d relates to a finite world, see Appendix I.)

---

[3] IBID: p. 144
[4] IBID: P. 172

Divine Providence

Since G-d is the sole force vitalizing our reality; everything that exists or occurs reflects G-dly intent. There is no such thing as a "chance" or "coincidence." Even a blade of grass waving in the wind expresses G-d's intention at that moment.

The expression of G-d in the world is called Divine Providence or *Hashgocha Protis*. It is behind every act, no matter how small or how large.

Since G-d, by definition, is the Essence of Good (and every other attribute), everything G-d expresses that goodness.

How can we understand Divine Providence in a world that appears to be chaotic, if not at times, psychotic?

There are two ways to answer this: from our view and from G-d's.

Imagine that you are looking at the back of a needlepoint landscape. From this perspective, all you see is a collection of threads of various colors. Everything looks random. Then you turn the needlepoint around. Now you see how everything fits. Each stitch serves a purpose. If there was a stitch missing, the entire effect would be lacking.

Now let's flip the painting to the back. If you look closely, you may be able to make out a pattern and maybe a form. You might even be able to see relationships that were hidden.

Similarly, G-d "views" the picture as it is in the totality of existence. We mentioned before that every event and occurrence reflects G-d's intent. Furthermore, G-d's intent expresses itself in all three dimensions of our existence: time, space, and soul.

Yet there have been obvious occurrences throughout history that do not appear to be "good" by any definition we can imagine.

There have been individual tragedies, national tragedies, events that defy any attempt to understand them. All things are true *from our perspective*. Furthermore, any attempt to understand someone's suffering, G-d forbid, ends up as either a rationalization or justification. The fact is, we cannot justify another's suffering, nor should we. Instead, we must do everything in our power to alleviate it.

If see someone suffering, we must cry out and ask for Hashem's mercy, help the person in any way we can, and do acts of kindness and goodness on the person's behalf.

If, G-d forbid, we are in physical or emotional pain, we must look inside and try to learn something from the situation. Perhaps we are being given a challenge to overcome or perhaps G-d is helping us to correct some blemish that may have occurred either in this lifetime or another.

Whatever the cause, our response must be to plead for G-d's tender mercies, to improve our behavior, to increase in acts of goodness and kindness, and seek out the advice of a sage who relates to us and, therefore, can advise us properly.

The bottom line is that a creation cannot know its Creator, as the prophet Isaiah (55:8) relates, *"For my thoughts are not your thoughts, neither are your ways my ways," declares the L-rd.*

We must learn about Judaism and G-d to the point where we are certain that the Divine Plan represents the ultimate Good for everyone and everything involved, no matter how it may seem at the moment.

For example, a stranger walks into an operating theater and sees a masked gang "attacking" a person using sharp knives in calculating ways. He is profoundly disturbed and leaves the theater looking for someone to rescue the unfortunate fellow.

Five minutes later, a medical resident walks into the theater, sees virtually the same situation, and comes to a completely different conclusion. The resident may not understand what the surgical team is doing. Nevertheless, he knows that the lead surgeon has the patient's best interests, if not his very survival, at heart.

If you find looking at things from the perspective of Above to below challenging, you are not alone. The Talmud records that once, Rabbi Joshua ben Levi joined Elijah the Prophet on his journeys. The two men visited the home of an elderly husband and wife who had an old milk cow. Poor as they were, the couple shared what they had with their guests.

Later, Elijah the Prophet and Rabbi Joshua ben Levi rose to leave. However before departing, Elijah the Prophet prayed to G-d and the cow died. Rabbi Joshua ben Levi was incensed. "Why," he questioned, "did the couple have to lose their only source of milk?" He demanded an explanation and received this answer: the time had come for the wife to pass away. Through his prayer, Elijah the Prophet interceded and death was decreed upon the cow, instead.

From the perspective of Above, the couple had sustained the lives of others, so their lives were sustained. They were rewarded measure for measure. From the perspective of our world below, however, it appears that their good deed was ignored and they suffered the loss of their cow.

In fact, the Talmud records dozens of instances in which the righteous have questioned the ways of G-d. Ultimately, they realized that our perspective is limited by time and our view of reality. G-d, however, is above time and beyond our understanding. You can be sure that:

a) G-d is good.

b) G-d is aware of every act or deed that a person performs.

c) Whether in this life or the next, every deed will be counted.

d) With the revelation of *Moshiach*, we will come to recognize the Divine Spirit that exists behind every event.

Why Did G-d Create this World?

Given G-d's Omniscience and Omnipresence, one could ask why did G-d create the universe? After all, He made it, and by definition, knows all that was, is and will be. Therefore, the existence of the world appears to serve no useful purpose to Him. So even it's no bother at all; still, why bother?

Once again, this question can be answered in several ways:

1. As we just mentioned, G-d is the Essence of Good, and it is the nature of good to do good. G-d's "nature" is to share His goodness (and other qualities). So G-d created the world so that *we* benefit. In essence, *we* are the purpose of creation.

2. *Midrash Rabba* (Nasso, Chapter 16) explains another reason for creating the world. *Nisaveh Hashem diro lo Yisborech b'tachtonim*, "G-d 'desired' to have a dwelling in the lower worlds." Desire is not necessarily rational. It could be. But, often, it is supra-rational. For example, as a kid, you probably wanted a special toy. Why did you want this particular toy and not that one? You may never know the "true" reason and, realistically, it does not matter. You had a craving for a particular object. Similarly, G-d had a "desire" to manifest his Presence (called *Shechina*) in the world below. There was no "logic." It was a desire, and as the Yiddish expression goes, *oif a taiva, freght nisht ken kashios*. "Regarding a desire, you can't ask questions."

3. From a slightly different angle, our sages say that there is no king without a people. A king surrounded by his relatives cannot be called a king. When we recognize and express our desire that the king rule, this elicits a similar response from the monarch. So, too, creation was formed as a crown for the Creator.

4. In a similar vein, G-d created Man to bring something novel into creation. Everything behaves according to rules that (to some extent) regulate their behavior. Man is the only creature that can

choose to do or not to do.[5] Whenever we freely choose to set aside our selfish desires for the sake of our Creator, this act causes gratification on high. At the same time, G-d allows our acts to help "perfect" the state that G-d made.

How do we know this?

At the end of describing the first six days of creation, the Bible states (Chapter II. Verse 3), "And G-d blessed the seventh day and sanctified it; because He rested from all His work that G-d created *to do*." The last two words do not add to the meaning. Rather, the words imply that something remains "to do." Our sages say what remains is man's duty to perfect himself and the world.

Kabbalah and *Chassidus* take this concept further, and explain that every one of us on Earth has a specific mission to perform. What's more, G-d gave each of us a unique set of talents and capabilities so that we can fulfill our mission. No one else can fulfill my task or yours, no one who lived before or who will live after. Not only that. Fulfilling our mission is necessary to establish a dwelling place for G-d on Earth.

To summarize, G-d is beyond our conception and comprehension. That is why the 10 Commandments began with the word, *Anochi*, meaning "I." The "I" (the Essence) of G-d is Unknowable. We can, however, come to recognize His existence by analyzing how G-d's being exists in man and the universe.

---

[5] Interestingly, we find this desire to have a person choose without compulsion mirrored in male-female relationships. We want our spouse to choose us for who we are, and not for any other reason. This also is one reason why G-d's reality is hidden from our view. If G-dliness were revealed, we could not but choose Him.

17

Words of Wisdom:

There is nowhere in the world devoid of the Divine Presence. (*Bamidbar Rabbah*)

You are far, farther than the heavens, and near, nearer than my body is to me. (*Kad Hakemach*)

G-d's essence is all-inclusive, unlimited, without any structure or additional qualities whatsoever. Every possible perfection exists in Him, but in an absolutely "simple (i.e., non-complex, non-composite)" manner. (*Ikkarim 2:9*)

For Further Reading:

The Light Beyond
Rabbi Aryeh Kaplan
Moznaim Publishing, 1981

Toward a Meaningful Life - The Wisdom of the Rebbe
Simon Jacobson
Morrow Publishers, 2004

The Way of G-d
Rabbi Moshe Chaim Luzzatto
Torah Classics Library, 2009

2. Man

Jewish philosophy looks at creation in terms of four categories. From the bottom up, the four categories are *domem* "inanimate," *tzomeach* "growing," *chai* "living" (i.e., animal life), and *m'daber* "one who speaks." Each level is incomparably higher than the one below it.

For example, earth and stones are inanimate. They do not appear to react to external forces such as heat or cold. They do not have the power of movement. In essence, their G-dly life force is totally hidden. Plants represent a higher level. Plants grow and have a limited amount of movement. Sunflowers, for example, will follow toward the sun. Animals are on a still higher level. They can certainly react to outside influences. They even have some power of expression and communication.

The highest level is man. As the "speaking one," man obviously has a number of capabilities. One of the most important is the ability to transcend, to go beyond one's self. The Bible alludes to this in the story of creation. When the Bible describes the creation of Adam, the first human, it uses the Hebrew word *vayeetzer*, "formed." In Hebrew, this word contains the letter *yud*, twice. When the Bible describes the creation of animals, *vayeetzer* is spelled with only one *yud*. According to our sages, this teaches us that both man and animals have a vitalizing soul, *Nefesh HaBahamis*. It consists of both intellectual and emotional qualities. In an animal, the emotional qualities control the intellect. It is called the *Yetzer Hara*, man's "selfish inclination."

In addition to the vitalizing animal soul, man also has a *Nefesh HaSichlis*, a soul capable of conceiving something beyond itself. It is the soul symbolized by the extra *yud* in *vayeetzer*. In man, the intellect can control one's emotions. For this reason, this soul is equated with the *Yetzer Tov*, man's "selfless inclination." This soul enables man to transcend his animal being by looking for something more than its immediate needs. For example, it is what leads man to moral, virtuous and ethical living.

Jews have another spiritual aspect, as well. It is called a *Nefesh Elokis*, a G-dly soul.[6] Like a flame that soars upward, the *Nefesh Elokis* yearns to merge with its Creator. Yet it cannot without ceasing to exist as an apparently independent entity.

To resolve this conundrum, G-d, in His kindness, G-d gave Torah and mitzvos. Learning the Torah enables us to unite with His wisdom. Our sages compare the Torah to spiritual nourishment for the soul. The soul becomes more sensitive and perceptive to G-dliness. Souls also require garments to enable them to

---

[6] (For a further explanation of the *Nefesh Elokis*, as well as how the powers of the soul reflect the dynamics of G-dliness, see Appendix II.)

experience G-dliness without being overwhelmed by it. *Mitzvos* serve as these "garments." When a person performs a *mitzvah*, he or she fulfills the Will of G-d. Since G-d is one with His Will, *mitzvos* enable man to access the highest aspects of G-dliness without becoming nullified the way a ray of light is nullified within the orb of the sun.

Gentiles do not have a *Nefesh Elokis*, they do; however, have the ability to unite with the Will of G-d. They achieve that unity by following the Seven Universal Laws that G-d gave to Noah and which were relayed by Moshe on Mount Sinai.[7]

At first glance, it seems Jews and non-Jews are "different." That is true, but different does not mean better. A non-Jew has one way of serving G-d. A Jew has another. It is by way of analogy, similar to two ladders. One ladder has seven steps. The other has 613. While the ladders are different, each ladder enables "the individual climber" to connect to G-d.

Still it appears that the Jewish people have been "chosen" to perform a particular mission. What does it mean to be chosen? To answer that question, let's turn to a letter from the Lubavitcher Rebbe, M.M. Shneerson, MHM:

---

[7] The Seven Universal Laws of Mankind, known popularly as the Noahide Laws are the foundation of just society:
1. Recognition of G-d, Prohibition of Idolatry
2. Recognition of the sanctity of life, Prohibition of Murder
3. Recognition of the value of society, Prohibition against Theft
4. Recognition of Divine Providence, Prohibition against Blasphemy
5. Recognition of the family unit, Prohibition against Immorality
6. Recognition of creatures, Prohibition against Eating the Limb or Flesh of a Living Animal7.
7. Recognition of the role of law, the Commandment to Promote Justice

..it is true that the soul of the Gentile and the soul of the Jew differ in their nature, this being connected with one of the basic principles of the Torah – the fact that the Jews are a people chosen from among the nations of the world. This chosen-ness originates in the fact that when G-d was about to give the Torah at Mt. Sinai, He first offered it to all the other nations of the world, who refused to accept it. The Jewish people did accept it. Needless to add, this is in no way inconsistent with the statement of our Sages, to the effect that righteous Gentiles have a special status and, according to the Rambam, also have a share in the World-to-Come.

Judging by your letter, it is surely unnecessary for me to emphasize to you what has already been indicated above, namely, that our belief in the chosen-ness of the Jewish people is not a matter of chauvinism or fanaticism, but rather the deep-felt realization that this uniqueness carries with it great responsibilities and special obligations. This is why, for example, Jews have to fulfill "*Taryag* (613) *mitzvos*," whereas Gentiles are not obligated to observe *kashrus* and various other restrictions....

Jew or non-Jew, each person has a job to do; one that only he can perform. Every job involves rising above his animal nature and selfish desires.

According to *Kabbalah* and *Chassidus*, man's unique ability to transcend is reflected in the fact that we walk erect. An animal walks on all four legs to indicate that its intellect and emotion are on the same level, and indeed, its intellect is controlled by its instinct and emotions. Walking on two legs, by contrast, enables man to look up and beyond his immediate environment and use his intellect a) to access the G-dliness that surrounds him b) to control one's vitalizing and instinctive/animalistic natures, and to use them to serve G-d the way a farmer uses an ox to plow a field.

Free Will = Controlled Responsibility

When many people think of "Free Will," they assume it means the ability to act without constraints or consequences. Unfortunately, that definition causes people to feel that they have the right to do what they want, when they want, and to whomever they want. In essence, free will is a license to do whatever "feels good."

Judaism takes a much deeper and much more demanding look at free will. Free will is the ability to choose to align (or heaven forbid, not align) our thought, speech, and deed with G-d in any situation we find ourselves.

We can exert control over our thoughts, our words, and our deeds. We can decide whether or not to dwell on or contemplate about a particular thing, speak about someone, or act in some way. If we knowingly choose, we are exerting our free will. If we react, we are not following our free will, but obeying our instincts and desires.

For example, if we're hungry and we eat, we do not necessarily express free will. When an animal is hungry, it eats.

However, if we're hungry and we postpone eating to perform some good deed or we give our meal to someone who is needy, we have transcended our natural desire to eat at the moment. This is not asceticism. We will eat, but we will decide upon the time, place and intent behind the act, not our natural inclination.

Furthermore, exerting free will means ensuring that every idea that we contemplate, word, and deed meets the Torah's code of behavior. If it doesn't, we will actively refrain from thinking, speaking or acting that way.

Probing deeper, free will means that we have applied our intellect to reign in and control our emotions and transcend our personal desires for good as defined by the Torah and our sages.

If we gave into our passions; or even worse, if we use our intellect to full our selfish desires, we have not exhibited free will. We abandoned our free will. Instead, we have blindly followed the fundamental drives of man for food, shelter, procreation, control/power, and pleasure. From that point, it's only a matter of time before the person rationalizes all his behaviors.

It is possible for a person to rationalize his behavior and still live an ethical life, yet as the Germans proved in World War II, it is also possible for one to fall lower than the lowest of animals.

Fortunately, even a person who focuses on his own selfish desires can change. In some cases, G-d arranges for an individual or event to affect our lives and help us turn things around. Sometimes, we have to go through many experiences until we learn our lesson.

For example, a thief may believe that he can't or won't be caught. If he's caught once (and he's smart) he'll admit his mistake and will not repeat it. Sadly, he may have not learned the lesson and keep stealing until he is caught again. Hopefully, he may eventually regret his previous action to the point where, if he was faced with the opportunity to steal again. If he will overcome his inclination no matter how much he wants or needs the money, he has passed one test[8] Furthermore he will eventually receive a reward for his righteous act. Not only that, he has overcome his desires and added something "novel" to creation.

All this is very nice, but often, we don't intend to commit a "sin." Instead, we are "led astray" by companions (...you can't really call them friends) or by circumstances beyond our control. The non-Jewish world calls this force of evil, Satan. In their view, Satan battles G-d for control of the universe. Judaism rejects this rather simplistic view of good and evil. G-d is the only force in the universe. Nothing else exists outside of G-d. Therefore, nothing can "battle" G-d for control of the universe. Judaism teaches that G-d created the concept of "evil" (or more accurately, G-d created an adversary/adversarial situation) to give us the opportunity to overcome it.

If we empower our *yetzer tov* (selfless inclination) to control our *yetzer hara* (selfish inclination), we have exerted our free will. If we actively perform a *mitzvah*, we actually "create" a good angel (i.e., positive energy).

If we follow our selfish inclination and commit a misdeed, G-d forbid, we "create" a bad angel (negative energy).

Eventually, a Heavenly evaluation is made. Do we deserve a reward for the *mitzvah* that we did? What type of reward? Do we deserve to go through some type of negative consequence as the result of a transgression? What type of consequence? Eventually,

---

[8] The Hebrew word for "test" is *nisayon*, which is similar to the *nes*, meaning the mast of a ship. Our sages teach us that a test is designed to elevate us the way a mast places a sailor on a higher level so that he can view of the ocean.

the Heavenly "court" comes to a decision and the appropriate reward or consequence is decreed from Above.

In some cases, the reward is given in this life in the form of children, livelihood, or health. Alternatively, the reward can descend as any one or two of the three. The reward could also be delayed until the person reaches his spiritual resting place after his allotted time on earth has passed. The reward could even be passed to future generations in terms of blessings. A similar evaluation is made regarding the consequences of misdeeds.

The thing to keep in mind is *altz mit a cheshbon* "Everything is done with a precise calculation." Every good deed is rewarded, every misdeed is recognized.

After Life

The stereotypical view of Heaven is a pleasure palace, a reward that is not related to the behavior that caused it. Judaism looks at the *Olam HaEmes* (the World of Truth) as dwelling place for the soul in which a person is repaid, measure for measure, for one's activities in this world. The kind of reward and dwelling place that we receive is commensurate with the Torah we learned, the *mitzvos* we fulfilled, and thought, speech, and deeds of goodness and kindness that we performed in this world.

Needless to say, performing a good life leads to a "good portion" in the World of Truth. On the other hand, a life of selfishness leads to a portion that involves recognizing and repairing the negative results of one's misdeeds. Nevertheless, there is a fundamental disagreement between the Jewish and non-Jewish views of *Gehinnom* (literally, "the Valley of Hinnom, considered the Entrance to the Underworld") in other words, "hell."

In Judaism, there is no such thing as a permanent dwelling place in purgatory. It is a principle of Judaism that every Jew has a portion in the World of Truth. The only question is whether the individual has earned that portion, whether he or she earned their place by first going through *Gehinnom*.

Rabbi Yosef Wineburg, OBM, one of the leading teachers in Chabad today, explains the concept as follows:

> The purgatory (*Gehinnom*) where the soul is cleansed of the "stains" of sin so that it may enter Paradise to enjoy the radiance of G-d's glory, operates on the principle of "measure for measure," i.e., punishment in kind. Thus sins of commission caused by the heat of passion and lust are cleansed in a *Gehinnom* "of fire," while sins of omission, due to indolence and coolness (i.e., lack of fervor), are cleansed in a *Gehinnom* "of Snow.[9]"

It should be emphasized that we are not referring to physical fires or physical snow, rather everything is seen within the context of relating to the Reality (i.e., Presence of G-d).

In the case of one whose passions overcame him, he may come "face to face" with his actions in his life and be embarrassed for the evil he did or caused. If his mistake was not due to passion but indifference or intellectual antipathy, he may find himself "distant" from G-d's Presence.

---

[9] Wineberg, Rabbi Yosef, *Lessons in Tanya*, Kehot Publication Society, NY, 1987, p. 130.

No matter what caused the spiritual blemish, one's stay in *Gehinnom* is temporary. After the person has been purified, he/she can enter their proper dwelling place in the spiritual world of reward called *Gan Eden*, (literally) the Garden of Eden, meaning Heaven in the World of Truth.

Like most concepts in Judaism, the process of judgment in the Afterlife is not black or white. It is possible that one's judgment could be modified or mediated by deeds performed on his or her behalf by the children and friends who remain in this world, or by the deeds of one's ancestors. In addition, G-d's mercy is beyond description or understanding, and therefore could play a large part in the person's obtaining a place in Heaven.

If necessary, the person could even be returned to this world to repair what he did wrong. This is the concept of reincarnation. The Kabbalist Rabbi Isaac Luria[10] taught that every individual must fulfill all 613 *mitzvos* in thought, speech, and deed.[11] We continue to reincarnate until we have completed this task, thereby perfecting all 613 organs of our body and 613 aspects of our soul[12]. This is in addition to any specific task or goal that G-d may have assigned.

Where do we find a hint of reincarnation in the Bible? In Genesis 2:17, G-d tells Adam, "Of the Tree of Knowledge of good and evil, you should not eat of it; for in the day that you eat, you should surely die." The Hebrew phrase, "surely die" is a double

---

[10] Rabbi Isaac Luria (1534–1572), known as the Ari HaKodesh, was a master of Kabbalistic thought.
[11] *Tanya*, Kuntres Acharon, Essay 5

expression, *mus tamus*. If the Torah just wanted to present the punishment for eating of the Tree of Knowledge, it should have said, *tamus*, "you shall die." By using the expression *mus tamus*, the Torah is telling us something else: "you will die (once) and die again.[13]" In other words, you will die and you will live again in order to rectify the wrong that you did; and then you will die again. According to our sages, the idea of completing a job (either in the positive sense of doing a *mitzvah* or in the negative sense of rectifying a wrong deed) is one explanation why some people leave this world earlier than others. Someone who passes away (G-d forbid) "before his or her time" descended to this world for a purpose. Once the purpose was fulfilled, the person returned to the higher world to enjoy the reward. Fortunately for us, most sages agree that this process of fulfilling all 613 *mitzvos* through various reincarnations is nearing its end. In other words, we have gone through reincarnation enough times to be almost finished. The job of perfecting ourselves and the world at large will be completed through *Moshiach* (the Jewish Messiah).

Yet, why put the soul through all of this in the first place? After all, prior to coming into this world, the soul enjoys a reflection of the Divine Presence. What could be better? Our sages answer by pointing out that the soul's position in the spiritual realm is only due to the benevolence of G-d. We don't deserve to be there. We have done nothing to earn the right. The Zohar calls this situation "bread of shame." By placing the soul into a body, and giving it temptations and the ability to overcome them, G-d enables the soul to reach a much higher level than it could before descending

13 Horowitz, Yeshaya (1565-1630), Shnei Luchot HaBrit, P. Mishpatim

into this world. The position it achieves after its allotted time on Earth is not "bread of shame" but a reward it has earned.

The *Zohar* (*Zohar* II, p. 163a) offers a parable: A king desired to test the moral strength of his only son. He had a most charming and clever woman brought before him. Explaining to her the purpose of the test, he ordered her to try her best to seduce the crown-prince. For the test to be valid, the prostitute had to use all her charms and guile without betraying her mission in the slightest way. Any imperfection on her part would mean disobedience (to the king) and failure of her mission. While the prostitute uses all her seductive powers, she inwardly desires that the crown-prince should not succumb to them.[14] Our sages call the prostitute the *yetzer hara*, our selfish (evil) inclination. It seeks to undermine one's relationship with G-d by focusing on one's selfish desires. It is up to us to decide which we follow.

To summarize, G-d created Man to manifest His Goodness. He furthermore granted man the ability to make the finite world a fit place for the revelation of G-d. Jews accomplish this by following the Torah and performing *mitzvos*. Non-Jews perform G-d's will by being and doing good i.e., following the Seven Universal Laws of Mankind. Everyone is rewarded for their good deeds and, conversely, must correct any negativity, (G-d forbid).

---

[14] Zalman, Rabbi Shneur, Tanya, Kehot Publishing Society, 1973, p. 39

Words of Wisdom

The soul of man is the lamp of G-d. (*Mishlei* 20:27)

Wisdom is to the soul is as food is to the body. (Avraham Ibn Ezra)

The world couldn't exist even one hour without acts of kindness. (*Osios Rabbi Akiva*)

For Further Reading:

Lights Along the Way
Rabbi A. J. Twerski,
Mesorah Publications, 1995

The Knowing Heart
Rabbi Moshe Chaim Luzzatto,
Feldheim Publishers, 2003

Anatomy of the Soul,
Rabbi Chaim Kramer
Breslov Research Institute, 1998

3. Torah

The word "Torah" is related to the Hebrew word *horaah*, which means "instruction." It teaches us how to live in a holy way.

The Torah consists of five "books." *Beraishis* "Genesis" begins with Creation and describes the lives of the Patriarchs, *Avrohom* "Abraham," *Yitzchok* "Isaac," and *Yaakov* "Jacob." The second book is called *Shemos*, "Exodus." It describes the "birth" of the Jewish people through their sojourn in, and liberation from Egypt. *Shemos* also contains the Giving of the Torah on Mount Sinai. The third book, *Vayikra* "Leviticus" describes the life of the Jewish people in the desert and the service of the tribe of Levi in the *Mishkan*, "Tabernacle." The fourth book, *Bamidbar* "Numbers" continues the journeys of the Jewish people through the desert. The fifth book is called *Devorim* "Deuteronomy." It restates many events, and ends with the death of *Moshe*, "Moses."

The Torah contains 613 commandments that are incumbent upon each Jew. Fittingly, our sages state that the soul has 613 "organs," and the human body contains 613 parts. The Torah is the means of establishing a relationship between the infinite wisdom of G-d and finite man. Most of us know that Moses received the Ten Commandments on Mount Sinai. But the fact is, he received the entire Torah. It includes all five books, called the Written Law, as well as the Oral Law that is required to explain them.

For example, *Devorim* contains the commandment to wear "frontlets upon our eyes." These are commonly known as *tefillin* "phylacteries." But the Torah does not tell us what they should look like, how to make them, or how they should be worn. There are other instances where the Torah only hints to certain commandments. To complement the written Torah, Moses received an entire body of knowledge, the Oral Law, to fill in these "gaps."

Rabbi Yehuda HaNasi organized this information into the six orders of the *Mishna* to prevent the information from becoming lost throughout the Jews' journey in exile. Since Rabbi Yehuda HaNasi wrote in an abbreviated style, the sages recorded their tradition of learning the *Mishna* in the *Gemara*. Together, the *Mishna* and *Gemara* are called the *Talmud*.

When people speak of the "Bible," they are not only referring to the Torah and Talmud but to other sacred literature as well. In Hebrew, the Bible is known as the *Tanach*, an acronym for *Torah*, *Neviim* (Prophets), *Kesuvim* (Writings). Prophets consist of Joshua, Judges, Samuel, Kings, Isaiah, Jeremiah, Ezekiel, as well as 12 Minor Prophets. *Kesuvim* includes Psalms, Proverbs, Job, Song of Songs, Ruth, Lamentations, Ecclesiastes, Esther, Daniel, Ezra-Nehemia, and Chronicles.

The Bible (*Tanach*) is a treasure house of Divine wisdom. It teaches us the way that man should live and what happens if he follows his drives.

Toras Chaim

The Torah is called by several popular expressions. One of these is *Toras Chaim*, meaning the "Torah of Life." In other words, the Torah covers every facet of life, including:

Agriculture: "You shall not plant the vineyard with mixed seeds." (*Devorim* 22:9)

Business: "A perfect and just weight shall you have; a perfect and just measure shall you have." (*Devorim* 25:15)

Ethics: You shall love your neighbor as yourself. (*Vayikra* 19:18)

Civil Law: "If indeed the theft be found in his hand alive, whether an ox or donkey or sheep, he must pay double." (*Shemos* 22:3)

Marine architecture: "And this is how you shall make it: three hundred cubits (shall be) the length of the ark; fifty cubits, the breadth of it; and thirty cubits, the height of it. A light shall you make to the ark, and to a cubit shall you finish it upward; and the door of the ark shall you set in the side thereof, with lower, second, and third (stories) shall you make it.[15]" (*Beraishis* 6:15)

In other words, events in the Bible are not just "stories" of the past. They are also paradigms, allegories, and models for us to

---

[15] In 2001, a respected marine architect performed a computer-aided analysis of the ark using the Torah's specifications. To his amazement, he found that the ark met all current United States and international laws for an ocean going barge. http://www.asknoah.org/html/arkdesign.html

use in the present and the future. For example, Noah built an ark to protect himself from the floodwaters. So too, we must protect ourselves from influences that can overwhelm us.

Noah survived by building and entering an ark. The Hebrew word for ark, *teva,* can also mean a "word." According to the Baal Shem Tov, the Torah is telling us to seek refuge in the words of Torah. Those words will give us the strength and the protection we need to withstand the storms around us.

In a third example, the Book of *Shemos* describes the enslavement and liberation of the Jewish people from Egypt. The Hebrew word for Egypt is *mitzrayim.* It is related to the word for "limitations" which is *metzarim.* So in addition to describing the history and culture of the era, the Torah is telling us that we can liberate ourselves from our own limitations. Furthermore, the Torah is showing us how.

Yet there's another way we can answer the question of why the Torah "came down" in the form of events and relationships, rather than as a list of rules. According to our sages, "Hashem looked into the Torah and created the world." In other words (and in other worlds), the Torah is addressing very spiritual concepts. When the Torah materialized in a physical world, these spiritual concepts became "enclothed" in a very physical form.

For example, the *Mishna* (*Bava Metzia* 1:1) discusses the following case: "Two people came before a court holding a cloak. One says, 'I found it.' And the other says, 'I found it.' Or one says 'It is entirely mine.' And the other says, 'It is entirely mine.' Each shall swear that not less than one half of it belongs to him, and they shall divide the value (equally)."

According to *Chassidic* philosophy, the *Mishna* is interpreted differently in the spiritual realms. Since cloaks do not exist there, the *Mishna* is discussing two souls who have come before a court, each claiming to be responsible for a particular *mitzvah* that was performed down here. Each one wants the merit for the *mitzvah*. Ultimately, each swears to at least half ownership and the merit is divided between them.

To reiterate, the Torah is composed of many events, stories and commandments, so that it could be learned on different levels. Furthermore, the words of the Torah were given without vowels. This allows words to be read in many different ways. For example, the Midrash says, "It was taught by Elijah: Whoever studies Torah laws every day is assured of life in the World to Come, for it is said "*Halichos* (the ways of) the world are his (*Chavakkuk* 3:6). (Yet) Do not read *Halichos*, but *Halachos* (Torah Laws.)" In this instance, the sages added an additional reading to prove that studying the Torah's laws guarantees life in the world to come. The rule is that *al tikrei* adds, but does not replace the meaning.

Generally, the sages say that there are 70 facets to the Torah. However, on a practical level, they identify five levels of Torah. They correspond to five levels of creation and five levels of the soul. (See Appendices I and II for further information.)

The five levels of Torah are, from the bottom up: *Pshat* "the Simple Meaning," *Remez* "Allusion," *Drush* "Homiletical Interpretation," *Sod* "Secrets of Torah," and *Chassidus*, the "Path to Serving G-d." How do these levels relate to us?

In the essay "On the Essence of Chassidus," the Lubavitcher Rebbe, Rabbi Menachem M. Schneerson, shares the five levels as they apply to the prayer we say each morning upon wakening:

Modeh Ani Lifanecha	"I offer thanks before You,
Melech Chai Vikayam	Living and Eternal King,
Shehechezarti Bi Nishmasi	For You have returned/restored my soul
B'Hemla Rabba Emunsecha	With mercy, Great is Your faithfulness."

According to the *Pshat*, the simple meaning of the prayer, we thank G-d for returning our soul to us in the morning. You'll notice that G-d's name isn't mentioned. This is because we haven't yet purified our hands by washing. Once we have washed our hands in the prescribed manner and rinsed our mouth, we are ready to mention the name of G-d in prayer. Since *Modeh Ani* doesn't contain G-d's name, we can say the prayer upon waking.

According to the level of *Remez*, allusion, *Modeh Ani* hints to the resurrection of the dead. Our sages call sleep "1/60th of death.[16]" In this manner, restoring our soul every morning is similar to the

---

[16] Midrash Rabbah Genesis 17:7

resurrection of the dead. Just as we thank G-d for "restoring our soul within me", we also proclaim, "Great is Your faithfulness" that you will resurrect the dead in the (immediate.) future.

According to *Drush*, the homiletic explanation, G-d returns our soul to us every morning, and does not withhold it for any "debts" we owe to G-d. So too, we should not withhold an article or our help from anyone due to the "debts" or other obligations that the person may have to us.

According to *Sod*, the esoteric meaning, the "living and eternal king" refer to the *sefirah* of *Malchus* as it is united with *Yesod*. This indicates that the restoration of the soul comes from a particular spiritual level.

According to *Chassidus*, the path to serving G-d, we can say *Modeh Ani* before washing our hands because, according to the Rebbe, "all the impurities of the world cannot contaminate the *Modeh Ani* of a Jew. It is possible that a person may be lacking in one respect or another – but his *Modeh Ani* always remains perfect.[17]" This reflects the point of the soul that is totally connected to G-d.

We have just explained one brief prayer according to five levels. These same five levels of explanation can be applied to the entire Torah. While this certainly indicates the breadth and depth of Torah, you can still ask the question, how do we get from learning Torah to the do's and don'ts of Judaism?

---

[17] Schneerson, Rabbi M.M, *On the Essence of Chassidus*, Kehot Publication Society, Brooklyn, New York, 1978, p. 45.

The answer is the analytical tools needed to understand the Torah were given to Moses and handed down from scholar to scholar throughout the generations. This is what the *Ethics of our Fathers* (1:1) means when it states, "Moses received the Torah from Sinai, and transmitted it to Joshua, and Joshua to the Elders; and the Elders to the Prophets; and the Prophets transmitted it to the Men of the Great Assembly."

The chain of scholarship starts from the Torah and continues through the *Mishna, Gemarah, Rishonim* (early Rabbis such as Maimonides), *Acharonim* (later Rabbis), and flows down to the the qualified scholars who decide Jewish law today.

For example, the prayer of *Shema* is found *Devorim*, Chapter 6, Verses 4 – 7 state:

4. "Hear (i.e., Comprehend) O Israel, The L-rd our G-d, the L-rd is one.

5. And you shall love the L-rd your G-d with all of your heart, and with all of your soul, and with all of your might.

6. And these words (shall be) that I command you this day, shall be upon your heart.

7. And you shall teach them diligently to your children, and you shall discuss them when you sit in your house, when you walking along the way, and when you lie down and when you rise up."

According to these verses, we have a commandment to say "these words" at specific times. But the verses do not define "these words" or "when you lie down and when you rise up."

The *Mishna* records the Oral Law that was given to Moses along with the written Torah. It begins to add flesh to the bare bones of the commandment. The *Mishna* was written in a very concise form. The *Gemarah* expands upon it. Together, the *Mishna* and *Gemarah* are called the *Talmud.*

In addition to the *Talmud*, many sages have provided commentaries, which in turn, have been codified into Jewish Law. You can find an example of this chain of tradition in Appendix III.

It is no coincidence that the Torah is called *Toras Chaim*, the living Torah. The Torah gives us guidance, instruction, and ultimately meaning to our lives.

Toras Moshe

The Torah was given to the Jewish people through *Moshe Rabbeinu* ("Moses our teacher.") Our sages state that "*Moshe emes vSoraso emes*, "Moses is true and his Torah is true."

The Torah testifies that, "And there never arose a prophet since in Israel like *Moshe* ...." (*Devorim* 34:10) In fact, two of Maimonides' Principles of the Jewish Faith are:

- "I believe with perfect faith that the prophecy of *Moshe* our teacher, may peace be upon him, was true; and that he was the father of all the prophets, those who came before him, and those who came after.
- I believe with perfect faith that the entire Torah that is now in our hands is the same Torah that was given to *Moshe* our Teacher, may peace be upon him."

40

Some western religions try to mimic the role of *Moshe* but fail because they don't understand it. These religions believe that the prophet serves as a "gatekeeper." In other words, G-d is too far above mortal man to be involved with his needs. Therefore, He chose someone to represent Him. As G-d's personal representative, he has the power to grant or deny personal requests. So to reach G-d, you have to go through him (or her).

Judaism rejects this. Judaism teaches that every person is unique and has a special, personal relationship to G-d. When we pray, we pray directly to G-d, not to anyone or anything else. We are permitted to ask *Moshe* or any *tzadik* "righteous individual" or departed loved one to intercede on our behalf. However, we don't have to go to, or through, anyone.

Rather, *Moshe* served as a "facilitator." He helped people establish and strengthen their relationship with G-d. His dedication is why the Torah is called *Toras Moshe*.

There are other reasons, as well. For example, *Moshe* also showed us what a human being could achieve. For example, a person who always lived on the plains cannot grasp the height of the heavens in the same way as a person who lives near a mountain. The mountain is his yardstick. Similarly, *Moshe* is our yardstick. Studying *Moshe* helps us to understand how high we can spiritually reach, and how far above that G-d is.

Yet *Moshe*'s role goes beyond that of a model and mediator between G-d and the Jewish people. The *Zohar* calls *Moshe* the

Raya Mehemna. Most scholars translate this phrase as the "faithful shepherd." But according to *Chassidus*, it could also be translated as "a shepherd of faith." Moses nurtured and sustained the faith of the Jewish people in G-d.

According to *Kabbalah* and *Chassidus*, every generation has someone who contains a spark of Moshe; that person is the *Tzadik HaDor*, the "righteous person of the generation." He watches over the nation of Israel just as a shepherd watches over his flock, and intercedes with G-d on their behalf. The *Tzadik's* "job" is to see that you spiritually achieve as much as you can. His focus is on you, your needs, your growth, and your relationship with G-d. The *Tzadik's* job requires total humility and self-effacement. When G-d commands *Moshe* to liberate the Jewish people, he responds, "Who am I that I should go to Pharaoh? (*Shemos* 3:11)" In addition, the Torah testifies, "And the man *Moshe* was exceedingly humble" (*Bamidbar* 12:3). *Moshe* was the paradigm of the *Tzadik*. This is another reason why the Torah is called *Toras Moshe*.

Toras Emes

The third expression is *Toras Emes,* the Torah of Truth. The Hebrew word *Emes* is spelled *aleph, mem, sof*. These are the first, middle, and the last letters of the Hebrew alphabet. This teaches us that truth is consistent from beginning to end. The Torah has that quality. It is consistent with its own set of rules from the first word in the Book of *Beraishis* to the last word in the Book of *Devorim*. It is also very, very subtle. As we saw earlier with regard to the word *vayeetzer*, in the creation of man, and as we'll see now, slight changes in spelling can indicate profound concepts.

Interestingly, modern science supports the Torah's view of creation. First, there was water, then plants, then animals, and, finally man. The "Big Bang" theory of the creation also is consistent with the Torah. The first sentence of the Torah is *Beraishis bara Elokim es hashamayim v'es haaretz*. It is usually translated as "In the beginning G-d created the heavens and the Earth." Translating it as accurately as we can, it reads. "The beginning (of creation) was produced by the Divine power that relates to nature, which first created *hashamaym* and then created earth." The word *hashamaym* is usually translated "heaven." But it actually combines two words *aish* "fire" and *mayim* "water." In essence, *hashamaym* describes a hot gaseous nebula. According to the Torah, this nebula represented the process of beginning. It then cooled and formed the planet Earth.

There are many, many other secrets hidden in the Torah. The keys to unlocking the secrets are the 22 Hebrew letters of the alphabet. The 22 Hebrew letters represent Divine channels of energy. Through these letters, creation came into being. In fact, *Kabbalah* and *Chassidus* compare the Hebrew letters to naturally occurring stone, while the letters of other languages are compared to bricks.

In 2007, Dr. Haim Shore, published *Coincidences in the Bible and in Biblical Hebrew*[18] which provides stunning examples of how Hebrew words describe the physical attributes of those

---

[18] Shore, Haim, *Coincidences in the Bible and in Biblical Hebrew*, iUniverse, Inc., 2007

words in ways that simply could not have been known thousands of years ago. Here are just two of the examples he gives:

The Hebrew word for "water" is *mayim*, spelled *mem, yud, mem*. There are two interesting aspects of the word. First, *mayim* is plural. Second, the word ends with the suffix *yim*. It indicates balance or symmetry. For example, *einyim* are "eyes. *Yadayim* are "hands", etc. Where is symmetry found in water? Obviously, the Hebrew word is symmetrical, *mem, yud, mem*. But the molecular structure of water is also perfectly symmetrical, H_2O. So the Hebrew word *mayim* describes the physical nature of water—it is made up of molecules in a symmetrical structure.

Similarly, the word for "ear" is *ozen* or in the plural *oznayim*. The Hebrew word for balance scales, *moznaim,* contains the same root. In other words, the Hebrew words are hinting to the relationship between the ear and balance. Yet it wasn't until the 18th century that scientists linked balance to the inner ear canal.

Was Man Formed from Dust?

Most people know of the Bible's description of the creation of man, in which Adam was formed from the dust of the earth. According to "science," this sounds unrealistic. Yet an article appearing in the Providence Journal in 1985 contained the astonishing headline, "Hallowed clay may be the key to the origin of life, after all." The story reported on the findings of chemists at NASA's Ames Research Center. The team of chemists demonstrated that ordinary clay can "store energy, transfer it from one region to another, and release it in a different form."

This research complements the findings of experiments, according to the article. It goes on to state:

[Previous research has shown that] "crystal-like patterns in clay can also undergo a rudimentary form of growth and self replication, two other fundamental life processes. This suggests, according to the researchers, that clay may have formed a kind of "proto-life" [by] providing a molecular pattern that helped to bring about the appearance of the first living cells.

The theory also evokes the biblical account of the Creation. In Genesis, it is written: "And the L-rd G-d formed man of dust from the ground," and in common usage this dust is called clay....[19]"

Perhaps the greatest testimony to the truth of Torah is the existence of the Jewish people. As a nation, the Jewish people are over 3,300 years old. What's more amazing is that we have remained a distinct people without the benefit of living in our own land. Even on foreign soil, even under political and economic pressure, Jews have remained true to the Torah. If man made the Torah, both it and Judaism as a way of life, would have faded away long ago. Only something beyond the social and political forces of the world could enable this tiny people to thrive as a lamb among 70 wolves.

There's another aspect. Virtually every religion was started by an individual who claimed some type of revelation. This individual shared his knowledge with disciples who taught the masses.

---

[19] The Providence Journal, April 3rd, 1985, P. A1-A2.

G-d gave the Torah to the Jews, through Moshe, on Mount Sinai, the 6th of Sivan in the year 2448. More than 600,000 men between the ages of 20 and 60 experienced this revelation. So did their wives and children. In addition, many non-Jews who had left Egypt with the Jewish people also experienced it. In fact, according to our sages, over three million people witnessed the giving of the Torah. They transmitted what they saw to their children and their children's children, down through the generations, without exception down until today. [20]

Interestingly, none of the nations of the world dispute this fact. They don't dispute the fact that the Jews were slaves in Egypt, either. If there are objections to the historical truth of Torah, they typically concern the miracles that took place either in Egypt or at the Sea of Reeds. For example, many people debate the fact that the sea split and drowned the Egyptians. But the fact is, if G-d created nature, then He certainly could change or modify it according to His will.

However, G-d could have as easily ordained that the splitting of the Sea of Reeds take place in a "natural way." For example, Israeli oceanographers Natan Paldor and Doron Nof,[21] used a computer to model a "wind set down" in which a steady flow of wind over shallow water causes it to move to the sides[22]. The point is that there are many ways to determine the truth of the

---

[20] For an exposition of the historical and spritual verity of Judaism, check out http://www.dovidgottlieb.com/publications.htm
[21] "Are There Oceanographic Explanations for the Israelites Crossing of the Red Sea?" Bulletin of the American Meteorological Society (Volume 73, no. 3, 1992)
[22] The examples provided are just to show how the Torah's descriptions do not necessarily contradict science. As Jews, we should not rely on such rationalizations or search for "scientific" explanations to reconcile the text with society's "enlightened" views.

Torah. But the only way that one can truly understand that truth is to live a life according to its dictates.

Words of Wisdom

Ben Bag-Bag said: "Turn it over and turn it over (the Torah), for everything is there. And look into it, and become grey and old over it; do not stray from it; for you have no better standard of conduct (*Avos* 5, *Mishna* 21)

The Torah is called peace, as it states, "Its ways are pleasant ways and all its paths are peace." (*Mishlie* 3:17)

There is no end to the Torah. Its measure is broader than the earth and wider than the sea. (*Iyov* 11:9)

For Further Reading:

Torah Studies
Rabbi Johnathan Sacks
Kehot Publications Society, 1996

The Torah Anthology–Meam Loez (Series)
Moznaim Publishers, 1979

Metsudah Chumash with Rashi
Rabbi Avronom Davis
Metsudah Publishers, 1999

4. Mitzvah

The term *mitzvah* means "Commandment." However, the word is connected to the phrase '*tzavtza v'chibur*, which means "Connecting and joining." A *mitzvah* connects the One who commands (G-d) with the one who obeys (man). A *mitzvah* expresses the Will of G-d. By performing the *mitzvah*, the soul is able to unite with the Will of G-d and still continue to exist. In essence, the *mitzvah* is a garment for the soul.

The most well-known *mitzvos* of all are expressed in the *aseres hadibros*, "the 10 Commandments." The 10 Commandments are found in *Shemos*, Chapter 20, Verses 1-14:

1. I am the L-rd your G-d Who has taken you out of the land of Egypt from the house of bondage.

2. You shall have no other gods before Me.

3. You shall not take the Name of the L-rd your G-d in vain.

4. Remember/Observe the Sabbath day to keep it holy.

5. Honor your father and mother.

6. You shall not murder.

7. You shall not commit adultery.

8. You shall not steal (kidnapping a person and selling that person into slavery).

9. You shall not bear false witness.

10. You call not covet.

These commandments were written on tablets and given to Moses on Mount Sinai. But they hint to, and include, many other commandments in the Torah[23]. In all, the Torah contains 613 *mitzvos*. There are 365 *negative mitzvos* (you shall not...) and 248 *positive mitzvos* (you shall...). The 365 negative commandments correspond to 365 blood vessels in the body. The negative commandments also correspond to the 365 days of the solar year. Fulfilling a negative commandment purifies the body and elevates it to a higher level of holiness.

The 248 positive commandments correspond to 248 bones (sections) in the human body. Fulfilling a positive commandment strengthens and enhances the relationship of the body and soul to the Creator. In addition to the 613 *mitzvos* found in the Torah, there are seven *mitzvos* of the sages. They were decreed to enrich our relationship to G-d. The seven are:

---

[23] *Mitzvos* fall into three broad categories: *Edus* means "Testimonies." *Edus* recall or testify to a particular event. For example, the holiday and commandments associated with Passover testify to the Exodus from Egypt. *Mishpotim* means "Judgments." *Mishpotim* include civil laws and commandments that we could have developed on our own. *Chukim* are "Decrees." We don't really know the reason for the commandment, but since G-d gave it, we must fulfill it. *Chukim* include the commandment to keep kosher and the commandment to use the ashes of the Red Heifer to cleanse one from the spiritual impurity caused by contact with the dead.

1. Lighting candles before *Shabbos*
2. Celebrating *Chanukah*
3. Celebrating *Purim*
4. Ceremoniously washing hands before eating bread
5. Making a blessing before eating or drinking and for certain occasions
6. Saying *Hallel* (psalms of praise) on holidays
7. Turning a public domain/area into a private domain/area using a technique called an *eruv*

The total number of commandments is 620. By Divine Providence, the Torah section containing the 10 commandments has 620 letters. Most of the 613 commandments only apply when we have the Holy Temple, a King and sovereignty over biblical Israel. Others only apply to a king or high priest. As a result, only about 270 *mitzvos* apply today. Both men and women are obligated to perform these commandments. However, women are exempt from performing positive *mitzvos* that are associated with a specific time. For example, women are not obligated to wear *tzitsis*, (ritual fringes) because, according to the letter of the law, *tzitsis*, are only worn during the day.

There are, nevertheless, three positive *mitzvos* that have a special connection to women (although they apply equally to men): the *mitzvah* to separate a portion of dough to recall the portion that was given to the priests; the *mitzvah* of lighting candles before *Shabbos* and *yom tov* (holidays); and the laws regarding family purity. If there is a woman in the house, it is she, not her husband, who makes sure that the *challah* dough has been set aside, that the Shabbos lights have been lit, and that she has immersed herself in a *mikvah* at the proper time.

The Value of a Mitzvah

Once upon a time, two souls met each other at a crossroads. One was going to Heaven, the other was going to a body on Earth.

"Tell me," the *Neshoma* on his way to this world asked, "What is it really like down there?"

"The world is a place where, once you earn a few kopecks (Russian coins), you can do a *mitzvah* and connect to G-d," replied the *Neshoma* on his way up.

The *Neshoma* on his way down rejoiced. "All it takes is a few kopecks to connect to G-d? That's fantastic." And he rushed down to his new home in a body.

The *Neshoma* on his way up sighed, "Just wait until he sees what it takes to earn a few kopecks."

Virtually all the *mitzvos* deal with physical things. For example, women need to physically kindle *Shabbos* lights. Men must wear *tefillin* weekdays. The idea is that these *mitzvos* not only connect G-d to man, they also elevate the physical world, thereby preparing it to be a fit dwelling place for G-d's presence. The act (whether it is in speech or deed) is called the "body" of the *mitzvah*. However, *mitzvos* also have a "soul" and that is the intention behind it. For example, we can put on *tefillin* while half-asleep and mumbling the words of prayer. Did we perform the *mitzvah* of wearing *tefillin*? Yes. On the other hand, we can concentrate on the meaning of *tefillin* as we don them and remind ourselves of their significance often during prayer. That's an entirely different experience and receives a correspondingly different reward.

The intention behind any act is called the *kavana*. One can have an intellectual awareness of the *mitzvah* and its meaning, or an emotional desire to connect with G-d, or ideally, both. What wings are to a bird, love and awe (through understanding G-d's greatness) are to a *mitzvah*. The more intention or *kavana* that you have, the "higher" the *mitzvah* goes in the heavenly spheres and the greater its ability to draw down Divine light and blessing. (See also *Kavana* in the chapter on Prayer.).

Men and Women: Their Roles within Judaism

Some women feel that not having as many opportunities to fulfill G-d's commandments is some sort of discrimination. Perhaps it is, but not in the way they think. Throughout Jewish literature, we find an interesting consistency. In the morning blessings many women say, "Blessed are You, L-rd our G-d, King of the universe, who made me according to Your Will." In *Tana D've Eliyahu*, we find, "Who is a proper wife? One who works her husband's will." Shlomo HaMelech calls the woman, the "crown of her husband."

The theme that connects is the concept of *Ratzon*, Will. In the G-dly spheres and in human beings, Will is associated with a level *above and beyond* intellect. One example is women's intuition. It is a feeling that may not be connected to anything apparent. It may even be contrary to surface appearances. Yet it often describes what turns out to be an emerging state of reality. This talent for intuition has an interesting implication. In Judaism, a woman cannot ordinarily serve as a judge in a legal case. According to Rabbi A.J. Twerski, the renowned psychiatrist, the reason is because they *intuit* who is innocent or guilty before any evidence is presented.

The contemporary *kabbalist* and scholar Rabbi Yitzchak Ginsburgh calls this level of *Ratzon*, "the source of all superconscious experience.... the force that propels one into consciousness...[24]"

Men, by comparison, are typically bound within the confines of reality. They express themselves through *Chochmah*. According to Ginsberg, *Chochmah* is "the innovative force that produces spontaneous insights...which serve to spark subsequent pursuit of meaningful knowledge." Men typically have a reason for everything they do or say. They focus on an objective. When they communicate, it's generally to give information.

By commanding men to perform *mitzvos*, G-d has enabled men to access the Divine Will that is more accessible to the feminine psyche. At the same time, many of the *mitzvos* and customs (e.g., wearing a yarmulke, *tefillin*, etc.) that men perform serve to remind them of their limitations (i.e., egos) and to encourage them to recognize their Maker.[25]

The point is, Judaism recognizes both male and female qualities and addresses them as equal yet different partners with G-d in perfecting the world. That perfection is achieved by being holy.

Jewish Dress and Appearance

As we mentioned earlier, the Hebrew word for "holy" (i.e. sacred) is *kadosh*. However, the word really means "set apart" or "dedicated to." We demonstrate that dedication and commitment

---

[24] www.inner.org

[25] Women, like men, are obligated to fulfill all negative commandments. They also "adopted" a number of positive commandments such as hearing the shofar. In addition, there are three positive commandments that apply—*challah*, *Shabbos* candles and *mikva*. The *kabbalistic* reasons behind these *mitzvos* are beyond the scope of this work, but they are very possibly linked to a level that is even higher than *Ratzon*, This level is called *Taanug* (Delight.)

to G-d by following the Torah's code of behavior and conduct. The Torah's laws help us fulfill our role as representatives of "a Higher Authority." Sadly, these codes are often at odds with the forms of behavior accepted by so-called "modern" societies.

The bottom line is that the Torah (*Vayikra* 19:2) calls on us to be holy because G-d is holy. The Talmud and rabbinic codes explain how men and women should fulfill that directive. In general, this standard of conduct requires Jews to avoid ostentation (i.e., self-aggrandizement) whether in speech, dress or deed.

In practical terms, clothes should not be revealing, particularly loud, or in any way call attention to oneself. Rather, one's clothes should be modest in keeping with Jewish tradition. This not only applies to women, but equally to men—even if the community maintains a different standard. The following analogy will, hopefully, put this in perspective.

Imagine you were assigned to represent your country in an important matter. You obviously would dress and act in a way that would reflect well on those you represent. This is especially true if you knew that, initially, you would be judged by your dress. As a Jew, you represent the King of Kings. Therefore, your dress, should reflect this. The same goes for your physical appearance.

In addition to wearing appropriate clothes, Jewish men and women have their own set of standards in terms of appearance.

For example, married Jewish women cover their hair. The fact that a woman's hair can be extraordinarily appealing is found in the Song of Songs (4:1), which states, "You are beautiful, my love, you are beautiful. Your eyes are dove-like behind your veil; your hair is like a flock of goats, trailing down from Mount Gilead." In addition to the verse indicating that a woman's hair should be covered, King David wrote in Psalms (45:15) "the great honor of the daughter of a King is hidden within," which stresses modesty as a feminine ideal.

As is usual, there is a lot more to the issue than meets the eye. According to Chassidus and Kabbala, hair is associated with the attribute of *gevurah* or "severity." (On a very mundane level, the life force in hair is so constricted that cutting it does not cause pain.) Interestingly, women are also identified with *gevurah* or *din*, "judgement."[26] Too much *gevurah* can affect the revelation of blessings in the areas of health, livelihood, or children. Covering the hair "tempers" the *gevurah* so that the blessings confront fewer obstacles. Obviously, covering one's hair does not guarantee abundant blessings. However, it is known that the Lubavitcher Rebbe (and other great sages) would state that, in addition to being Jewish law, covering one's hair helps obtain revealed blessings in the areas of *parnossa* and children.

Men also cover the head with a skullcap to indicate one's acceptance of the Kingdom of Heaven. In fact, the word for skullcap, *yarmulke*, may be a derivation of the Hebrew words, *yira malka*, "fear of heaven."

In addition to wearing a *yarmulke,* males are encouraged to keep their hair short. There are several reasons for this. On a practical

---

[26] The association between women and *gevurah* is not negative. On the contrary, this attribute tempers the attribute of *chesed* "kindness" and vice versa, so that the outcome is positive. This may be why our sages say, "Women are the source of blessing in the house."

level, the *Tefillin shel Rosh* is supposed to rest on the top of the skull, between the eyes. Having a lot of hair interferes with fulfilling this precept and makes it easy for the *Tefillin Shel Rosh* to slip out of place.

There's another reason for men to have short hair. Having long hair may be forbidden under the precepts of not dressing like a woman (*Devorim* 22:5) or following the ways of a non-Jew. (*Vayikra* 18:3, 20:23) Long hair is also associated with ego, which prevents a person from serving Hashem properly. Furthermore, the *gevurah* associated with hair can become manifest in negative ways. For example, everyone knows the basic story of Samson who was endowed with superior strength. As the events are found in Judges, Samson's strength "grew" from keeping the locks of his hair uncut. The problem was that, in addition to physical strength, Samson had uncontrollably strong desires in other areas, which led to his downfall. Whether or not they are like Samson, men should still have short hair.

Short hair is one mark of a Jewish male. Having a beard is another. The commandment for men not to trim the beard is found in *Vayikra* 19:27:28, "You shall not trim your hair at the temples or mar the edges of your beard."[27] The prohibition against shaving may also associated with Torah commandments banning men dressing like a woman and/or following the lifestyles of non-Jews, and especially idol worshippers.

---

[27] Interestingly, the Torah continues, "You shall not lacerate your bodies for the dead or tattoo any marks upon yourselves." The Torah not only forbids tattoos on any kind for men and women, it links tattoos with idolatrous practices.

From a more esoteric perspective, the beard is a revelation of something that was previously hidden. According to our sages, Hashem has 13 strands in His beard. They correspond to the 13 Attributes of Mercy that G-d used to initiate creation. For that reason, a beard is associated with *rachamim* or "mercy." The story is told of a man who came to the 19th century rabbi, Shlomo Klugar. The man said that he and his wife had children, but that they did not survive infancy. He asked the rabbi for advice. Rabbi Kluger replied, "A baby naturally grabs his father's beard. Since you have no beard, your children have nothing to hold. Let your beard grow and your children's lives will be sustained." The man followed Rabbi Kluger's advice and he and his wife were rewarded with healthy children.

The prohibition of cutting the corners of the beard traditionally applies to the use of a straight razor, not to scissors that don't "shave" the skin. For that reason, some rabbis permit shaving with an electric shaver. However, many of today's electric shavers lift the beard and cut it so close to the skin that the effect is similar to a razor. If a person has a question, he should discuss the matter with an Orthodox rabbi.

What about permanent "body art?" The Torah (*Vayikra* 19:28) states, "Do not put tattoo marks on yourselves, I am the L-rd." In other words, a person's body is not his/her own. It is the property of G-d and G-d wants a person to remember that by reflecting the dignity of man's Maker.[28]

So far, we've covered how one looks. The concept of holiness also includes thought, speech and deed. Every thought represents energy. Positive thoughts emit positive energy. Negative thoughts emit negative energy. Holy thoughts emit holy energy. Ideally, a person should control his thoughts so that they are positive and holy. If a negative thought pops up, it should be pushed away. Unless you are a completely righteous person, you cannot bring positive results by dwelling on a negative thought.

Speech should also express holiness. The Torah prohibits slander, tale-bearing (even if true) and any negative speech—even positive speech is forbidden if it's to elicit a negative response.

Therefore the best policy is that if you want to criticize anyone, criticize yourself. If you want to praise someone, praise G-d.

Typically, holiness is expressed through humility, as our sages have said, "Where you find G-d's greatness, you find G-d's humility." The Torah testifies that Moshe was the most humble person who ever walked the earth. He was also aware of his accomplishments. However, he believed that, given the same background, any person could have achieved those accomplishments and perhaps exceeded them.

To put it another way, if a person feels that he is the center of his universe, there's no place for G-d. For example, a person can do

---

[28] If a Jewish person has a tattoo, he remains Jewish. He still has to perform all the mitzvos, including eating kosher, donning tefillin, etc. Even when he passes away, he should be buried in a Jewish cemetery.

mitzvos modestly without trying to attract attention or the same *mitzvos* can be performed with all the trappings of one's ego.

As much as possible, a person should always try to be as G-dly as possible by performing *mitzvos* and by emulating the ways of G-d in thought speech, and deed. Shlomo HaMelech (King Solomon) put it best when he wrote (Proverbs 3:6), "Know G-d in all Your Ways."

*Now **that's** humility.*

Rabbi Yosef Rosen (1858-1936) was known for his diligence in Torah study. Even as a young boy, he spent his time pouring over religious texts. It wasn't long before the teachers in his town of Rogotchov, Russia, said he was beyond them, so his father took over. When he was 13, his father brought him to Rabbi Yosef Dov Soloveichik and asked the renowned scholar to accept Yosef as a student. Rabbi Soloveichik asked the bar mitzvah boy if he was familiar with the 63 tractates of the Talmud. The lad replied that he knew half. "Which half?" Rabbi Soloveichik wanted to know. The boy let out a slight smile, "Which ever half you ask me."

Words of Wisdom

A little with devotion is better than a lot without. (*Shulchan Aruch, Orach Chaim* 1:4)

Three things were granted to Israel on condition they observed the commandments: The Land of Israel, the Holy Temple, and the Kingship of the House of David. (*Mechilta, Yisro*)

One act is better than a thousand sighs. (Rabbi Joseph Isaac Shneersohn)

For Further Reading:

Mishneh Torah (Series)
Maimonides, Translated by Rabbi E. Touger
Moznaim Publishers, 1998

Metsudah Kuzari, Rabbi Yehuda Halevi
Translated by Rabbi Avrahom Davis,
Metsuda Publishers, 1986

Lessons in Tanya
Rabbi Yosef Wineberg
Kehot Publication Society, 1998

5. Blessings

Ideally, everything we do should in some way be linked to G-d, as our sages say in Ethics of the Fathers, "Let all your deeds be for the sake of Heaven." Blessings help us achieve that goal. The Hebrew word for "blessing" is *bracha*, which is linked to the Hebrew word *bircav*, meaning "(bending through) the knees." *Chassidus* explains that the purpose of a blessing is to draw down G-dly energy from above. This is accomplished by physically saying the blessing loud enough that you can hear it yourself.

In general, blessings fall into three categories: blessings that are connected to the joy and satisfaction we receive from eating, drinking, and even smelling pleasant things; blessings that are associated with Divine commandments, and blessings that acknowledge G-d in all our affairs. In fact, we begin and end each day with a blessing.

Blessings Upon Rising

Every day is a gift from G-d. By saying the prayer of *Modeh Ani*, we thank G-d for the present of a present. While this prayer does not invoke the name of G-d, it is considered to be like a blessing.

Modeh Ani is the first thing we say when we open our eyes. We should say it while we are still in bed, even before washing our hands and rinsing our mouth:

Modeh Ani Lifanecha	"I offer thanks before You,
Melech Chai Vikayam	Living and Eternal King,
She'hechezarti Bi Nishmasi B'Hemla	For You have restored my soul in me with mercy
Rabba Emunasecha	Great is Your faithfulness."

According to our sages, the Jewish soul "reports the day's activities" to the world above. At this point, only a "residue" of life remains in the body. This is comparable to 1/60th of death. When the soul returns to the body, the spiritual impurity associated with this level of death remains on the fingertips. Therefore after saying *Modeh Ani*, and before getting out of bed, we wash *negel vasser*, "nail water." We first pour water over the right hand, then over the left, and repeat this pattern two more times to remove any spiritual impurity.

Once dressed, we wash in the same manner again. This time, we say the following blessing teaching us to dedicate our hands (i.e., actions) to serving G-d. (NOTE: We stand when saying the following blessings.)

Baruch Atoh Ado-noi Elo-heinu	"Blessed are You, L-rd our G-d,
Asher Kiddeshanu	with His commandments
B'mitzvosov Vitzivonu Al	commanding us regarding
Natilas yadaim	washing our hands."

We follow this with a number of blessings that correspond to various activities that occur next. In this way, we recognize and thank G-d for bestowing His many *brochos* upon us.

The first blessing acknowledges G-d's role in creating our physical body and the system that eliminates waste. Putting this blessing in perspective, Rabbi Tanchuma said, "If you stuck a pin in a balloon, the air will escape. Yet the human body has many holes that allow bad air and waste to leave, yet the good air and food still remain inside."

In addition to saying this blessing when we wake, we say it after leaving the bathroom and washing our hands in the manner described above:

Baruch Atoh Ado-noi Elo-heinu *Melech HaOlam*	"Blessed are You, L-rd our G-d, King of the universe
Asher Yatzar Es HaAdam	Who formed Man with wisdom

B'Chochma

Uvoro Bo Nkavim, Nkavim,	and created him with many orifices
Chalulim, Chalulim, Galui	and many cavities. It is revealed
V'Ydua Lifnei Kisei Cvodecha	and known before Your Throne of Glory
She Im Yesasaim Echad Maihem	that if one became blocked
O Im Yipaseach Echad Meihem	or if one opened
Ei Efshar L'hiskayem Afilu Sha'ah Echas	it would impossible to exist even for one moment.
Baruch Atoh Ado-noi Rofeh Kol Basar U'Mafli Laasos.	Blessed are You, L-rd, Who heals all flesh and performs wonders."

The following prayer is similar to *Modeh Ani* with two exceptions. It mentions the name of G-d. It also uses four expressions that correspond to the four "worlds" of creation. "The soul that you gave me is pure" refers to the highest world the World of Emanation. "You created it" refers to the World of Creation. "You formed it" refers to the World of Formation. "You breathed it" refers to the World of Action. (For a further explanation see Appendix I.)

Elo-hai, Neshama She'nasata Bi Tahora Hee	"My G-d, the soul that You gave me is pure
Atah Berasa, Atah Yetzartah,	You created it. You formed it.
Atah Nefachta Bi, V'Atah	You breathed it into me. You

M'Shamra b'kirbi	guard it in me.
V'Atah Asid Litla Mimeni	And eventually You will take it from me
U'lhachazira Bi L'asid Lavo	and return it into me in the Time to Come
Col Zman Sh'haneshma b'kirbe	All time the *Neshoma* is within me
Modeh Ani Lfanecha Ado-noi Olo-hai	I thank you, L-rd my G-d,
V'alohai Avoisai, Ribon Kol HaMaasim	and G-d of my fathers, Master of all deeds
Adon Kol HaNeshomos	L-rd of all souls.
Baruch Atoh Ado-noi	Blessed are You L-rd
Hamachazir neshamos lfgarim meisim.	Who restores souls to lifeless bodies."

After referring to the descent of the soul into the body, we thank G-d for the natural superiority of man. In the following blessing, *sechvi* means "rooster" and teaches us that G-d created the natural order of life. However, it also refers to "heart," i.e., one grasps the concept so thoroughly that he feels it in one's heart. In this context, we thank G-d for allowing us to tell the difference between light (good) and darkness (evil.)

Baruch Atoh Ado-noi Elo-heinu	"Blessed are You, L-rd our G-d,

Melech HaOlam	King of the universe
Hanosain L'sechvi Vina	who gives the rooster understanding
L'havchin Bain Yom Ubain Liela	to discern between day and night."

Similarly, the following blessing can be read on many levels. In it, we thank G-d both for sight and insight:

Baruch Atoh Ado-noi Elo-heinu	"Blessed are You, L-rd our G-d,
Melech HaOlam	King of the universe
Pokeach Ivrim.	Who opens the eyes of the blind."

When you are asleep, you are not in control of your movements. When you wake up, you take control of your body once more. For that reason, we say the following blessing:

Baruch Atoh Ado-noi Elo-heinu	"Blessed are You, L-rd our G-d,
Melech HaOlam	King of the universe
Matir Asurim.	Who releases the bound."

Most animals spend their lives facing the ground. In the following blessing, we thank G-d for enabling us to spend our lives in an upright manner, both physically and spiritually:

Baruch Atoh Ado-noi Elo-heinu	"Blessed are You, L-rd our G-d,
Melech HaOlam	King of the universe
Zokeif Kfufim.	Who straightens the bowed."

Just as a body needs clothes for beauty and protection, the Jewish soul must be clothed in words of Torah and good deeds. The following blessing thanks G-d for giving us this ability.

Baruch Atoh Ado-noi Elo-heinu	"Blessed are You, L-rd our G-d,
Melech HaOlam	King of the universe
Malbish Arumim.	Who clothes the naked."

Usually, when we go to bed, we are very tired. Yet we wake up feeling much better. The following blessing thanks G-d for renewing our feeling of strength and hope every day:

Baruch Atoh Ado-noi Elo-heinu	"Blessed are You, L-rd our G-d,
Melech HaOlam	King of the universe Who
HaNosain Lyaeif Koach.	Gives strength to the weary."

Most (2/3) of the Earth is covered by water. In the following blessing, we thank G-d for giving us dry land:

Baruch Atoh Ado-noi Elo-heinu	"Blessed are You, L-rd our G-d,

Melech HaOlam   King of the universe

Rokah HaAretz al Hamayim.   Who spread the earth over the
                                    waters."

The next blessing lets us thank G-d for the ability to walk. There
is, however, a deeper meaning to this blessing. Each of us has a
mission in life and G-d guides and directs us to perform that
mission through Divine Providence. When we recognize that G-d
is directing our steps from Heaven, we can feel much more secure
in this world.

Baruch Atoh Ado-noi Elo-heinu   "Blessed are You, L-rd our G-d

Melech HaOlam   King of the universe

Hamachin Mitzadei Gaver.   Who directs the steps of man."

The following blessing is "tied in" with shoelaces. It thanks G-d
for giving us what we need to go out and work, such as shoes.

Baruch Atoh Ado-noi Elo-heinu   "Blessed are You, L-rd our G-d,

Melech HaOlam   King of the universe

SheAsah Li Kol Tzarchi   Who has provided me with all my
                                    needs."

According to our sages, the next blessing refers to a belt or sash that separates the more animal parts of our body from the more spiritual. It also symbolizes our strong attachment to G-d.

Baruch Atoh Ado-noi Elo-heinu	"Blessed are You, L-rd our G-d,
Melech HaOlam	King of the universe
Ozer Yisroel B'Gevurah.	Who girds Israel with might."

The following blessing refers to our custom of wearing something on one's head. A head covering teaches us that G-d's wisdom is incomparably "above and beyond" our own.

Baruch Atoh Ado-noi Elo-heinu	"Blessed are You, L-rd our G-d,
Melech HaOlam	King of the universe
Oter Yisorel B'Sivara.	Who crowns the people Israel with glory."

The next three *brochas* recognize the differences that exist among people. For example, a non-Jew can eat and drink everything. A slave doesn't have to work for food, clothing, and shelter; his master supplies them. Women have a built-in sensitivity to spirituality and G-dliness. In each case, men must thank G-d for both the obligation and privilege of serving Him.[29]

---

[29] Rebbetzin Chaya Teldon views these three blessings as the source for thought-provoking questions. "I may not be a non-Jew, but am I living a Jewish life?" "I may not be a slave, but have I liberated myself from being a slave to our desires, habits, ways of thinking, etc.?" "I may not be a woman, but am I being a *mentch* i.e., acting the way a Jew should?"

Baruch Atoh Ado-noi Elo-heinu	"Blessed are You, L-rd our G-d,
Melech HaOlam	King of the universe
She Lo Asani Goy.	Who has not made me a non-Jew."

Baruch Atoh Ado-noi Elo-heinu	"Blessed are You, L-rd our G-d,
Melech HaOlam	King of the universe
She Lo Asani Oved.	Who has not made me a slave."

(Women do not say the following)

Baruch Atoh Ado-noi Elo-heinu	"Blessed are You, L-rd our G-d,
Melech HaOlam	King of the universe
She Lo Asani Isha.	Who has not made me a woman."

When we sleep, we aren't thinking. So things that are very silly can appear very real. In the same way, the *Yetzer hara*, man's selfish inclination can trick a person into erring; but only if that person is "sleeping" and not thinking about G-d. In this blessing, we thank G-d for removing sleep and we ask for His protection every day.

| *Baruch Atoh Ado-noi Elo-heinu* | "Blessed are You, L-rd our G-d, |
| *Melech HaOlam* | King of the universe |

HaMavir Sheina Me'Aeini	Who removes sleep from my eyes
Usnuma MaAfapai	and slumber from my eyelids."

We make the following *brocha* over the ability to understand G-d's Torah.

Baruch Atoh Ado-noi Elo-heinu	"Blessed are You, L-rd our G-d,
Melech HaOlam	King of the universe
Asher Kiddeshanu	Who has sanctified us
B'mitzvosov Vitzsivanu	with His commandments, commanding us
Al Divrei Torah.	concerning words of Torah."

The next blessing thanks G-d for giving us the written Torah.

Baruch Atoh Ado-noi Elo-heinu	"Blessed are You, L-rd our G-d,
Melech HaOlam	King of the universe
Nosain HaTorah.	Who gives the Torah."

Once we've made blessings over the Torah, we immediately recite some passages from it. In the next passage, Aaron and his sons, who are *Cohainim* (priests), are commanded to bless the Jewish people. This three-part blessing comes to us in the merit of our forefathers, Avraham, Yitzchok, and Yaakov.

V'yedaber Ado-noi el Moshe Laymore	"And the L-rd spoke to Moses, saying
Daber El Aaron V'el Banav Laymore	Speak to Aaron and to his sons, saying
Co S'varchu Es Bnai Yisroel,	'Thus, shall you bless the children of Israel
Amar Lahem: Y'vorech'checha Ado-noi	Say to them, 'The L-rd bless you and watch over you
V'Yishmarecha	and guard you.
Ya'er Ado-noi	The L-rd make His
Panav Aleicha Vichuneka.	Face shine upon you and grace you.
Yisa Ado-noi Panav Aleicha	The L-rd turn His Face to you
V'yaseim L'cha Shalom.	and grant you peace.
V'samo Es Shmi Al	And they shall set My name upon
Bnai Yisroel	the children of Israel
V'Ani Avarcheim	and I will bless them."

Blessings for Special Occasions

In addition to morning blessings, we make blessings over food and on special occasions and situations. For example, when we celebrate a major holiday, eat a new fruit, or in some way mark a milestone, we say the following blessing:

Baruch Atoh Ado-noi Elo-heinu	"Blessed are You, L-rd our G-d,
Melech HaOlam	King of the universe

73

SheHechiyanu V'kiyimanu,	Who has granted us life and sustained us
V'higianu L'zman Hazeh	And enabled us to reach this occasion."

Before smelling different spices, we say:

Baruch Atoh Ado-noi Elo-heinu	"Blessed are You, L-rd our G-d,
Melech HaOlam	King of the universe
Borei Minei Bsamim	Who creates various spices."

Over thunder, a hurricane, or an earthquake, we say:

Baruch Atoh Ado-noi Elo-heinu	"Blessed are You, L-rd our G-d,
Melech HaOlam	King of the universe
Shekocho U'gvuroso Malai Olam	Whose power and might fill the world."

Upon seeing lightning or shooting stars, we say:

Baruch Atoh Ado-noi Elo-heinu	"Blessed are You, L-rd our G-d,
Melech HaOlam	King of the universe
Oseh Maasai B'raishis.	Who re-enacts the work of Creation."

Upon hearing bad tidings, G-d forbid, say:

Baruch Atoh Ado-noi Elo-heinu	"Blessed are You, L-rd our G-d,
Melech HaOlam	King of the universe,
Dayan HaEmes.	the true Judge."

What Blessing?

Rabbi Nachman Raphael Kahan was exiled to Siberia for the "crime" of teaching Torah to children. After years of deprivation, he was finally allowed to return home. Entering the synagogue in Leningrad for the first time, a fellow Chasid approached him and said, "When people see each other after a long absence, they typically say the blessing, "*Shehechyanu*" marking the occasion. But what blessing do you say when you finally meet someone that you have heard about, but never met before?" The Chasid didn't wait for Rabbi Kahan to think of an answer, but said, "One takes a bit of whiskey, says "*L'Chaim!*" ("To life!"), and makes the blessing, "*Shehacol Neheya Bidvaro.*"

Upon hearing good tidings, say:

Baruch Atoh Ado-noi Elo-heinu	"Blessed are You, L-rd our G-d,
Melech HaOlam	King of the universe,
HaTov v'Hamativ	Who is good and does good."

There is a special blessing one says after recovering from a severe illness, after crossing the sea or desert, leaving prison, or being rescued from any other life-threatening situation. We only say it with a quorum (10 men) when the Torah is read.

Baruch Atoh Ado-noi Elo-heinu	"Blessed are You, L-rd our G-d,
Melech HaOlam	King of the universe,
HaGomel L'Chayavim Tovos	Who bestows goodness upon the culpable
Sh'Gmlani Tov.	for He has bestowed good upon me."

The Congregation responds:

Mi Sh'Gmalcha Tov	"May He Who has bestowed goodness on you
Hu YiGmalcha Kol Tov Sela	always bestow all goodness on you."

The previous blessing symbolizes a *Korbon Todah*, the "Thank Offering" that was brought in the Holy Temple. Therefore, it is customary to donate money to a worthy cause. This will demonstrate that just as G-d acted charitably to us, so will we act charitably to others.

Blessings Over Food.

Before eating and drinking, we make blessings to elevate our food or drink.

Bread is the staple of life. It is so important that 12 loaves were sanctified in the Holy Temple every week. Just as a Cohain had to elevate his hands prior to performing a sacred service, we pour water three times consecutively over the right hand, then three times over the left before eating bread.

After washing we say:

Baruch Atoh Ado-noi Elo-heinu	"Blessed are You, L-rd our G-d
Melech HaOlam	King of the universe
Asher Kiddeshanu	Who has sanctified us
B'mitzvosav Vitzivonu	with His commandments, commanding us
Al Natilas Yadaim	to wash our hands."

Over bread, we say:

Baruch Atoh Ado-noi Elo-heinu	"Blessed are You, L-rd our G-d,
Melech HaOlam	King of the universe
HaMotzie Lechem Min HaAretz	Who brings forth bread from the earth."

Over meat, fish, drink, eggs, mushrooms, and milk products, say:

Baruch Atoh Ado-noi Elo-heinu	"Blessed are You, L-rd our G-d,
Melech HaOlam	King of the universe
Shehacol Neyah Bidvaro.	By Whose word all things came to be."

Over fruit from trees, we say:

Baruch Atoh Ado-noi Elo-heinu	"Blessed are You, L-rd our G-d,
Melech HaOlam	King of the universe
Borei Pri HaAitz.	Who creates the fruit of the tree."

Over fruit and vegetables that grow from the ground, say:

Baruch Atoh Ado-noi Elo-heinu	"Blessed are You, L-rd our G-d,
Melech HaOlam	King of the universe
Borei Pri Hadama.	Who creates fruit of the earth."

Over cooked and baked dishes, cookies and cake made from wheat, barley, spelt, oats or rye, we say:

Baruch Atoh Ado-noi Elo-heinu	"Blessed are You, L-rd our G-d,
Melech HaOlam	King of the universe
Borie Minai Mezonos.	Who creates various kinds of food."

Over wine grape juices, we say:

Baruch Atoh Ado-noi Elo-heinu	"Blessed are You, L-rd our G-d,
Melech HaOlam	King of the universe

Borie Pri Hagafen.	Who creates the fruit of the vine."

Once we finish, we thank G-d for providing the food.

After eating fruit, meat, milk products or drank anything other than wine or grape juice we say:

Baruch Atoh Ado-noi Elo-heinu	"Blessed are You, L-rd our G-d,
Melech HaOlam	King of the universe
Borei Nefashos Rabos	Creator of many living beings
V'Chesronan Al Col Ma Shebarasa	and their needs, for all things You have created with which
L'hachaios Bahem Nefesh Col Chai	to sustain the soul of every living being.
Boruch Chay Haolamim.	Blessed is He Who is the Life of the worlds."

After eating cookies, cake, and fruits associated with the land of Israel (figs, grapes, dates, pomegranates), we say a brief blessing with three parts. You'll find it in a prayer book.

After eating bread, we say the full *bentching* (grace after meals) that is printed in a prayer book.

In general, if you're having a meal and you wash and say the blessing over bread, you don't have to make a separate blessing for each item that you eat. If you do not wash and eat bread, you should make a separate blessing for each type of item, e.g., fruit of the ground, fruit of the tree, crackers or cookies (*Borei Minai Mezonos*), meat, eggs, fish, etc. (*Shehacol*).

If you have several items of one group before you, (e.g., an apple and a pear) you would say one blessing *Borei Pri HaAitz* over both items. Similarly, saying one blessing *Shehacol* could include meat, fish, eggs or drinks (except wine or grape juice) etc.

Words of Wisdom

When the early Chassidim would say the blessing *Shehacol* (which is usually said over drink, meat, and milk products) they would also have "in mind" things that deserve a blessing, but never get one, e.g., music, joy, love, friendship, beauty, etc. (Heard from Rabbi A.J. Twerski)

Rabbi Meir states that a man should try to say 100 blessings every day. (*Tur Orach Chaim*) We typically accomplish this on weekdays, when we recite the three daily prayers. On *Shabbos* and holidays, our prayers contain fewer blessings. Therefore, we accomplish our quota of 100 blessings by going to the synagogue and saying "amen" when required.

Every soul should bless the L-rd (Psalm 150).

For Further Reading:

Abbreviated Code of Jewish Law
Translated by Rabbi E. Touger
Moznaim Publishing, 2004

To Be a Jew
Rabbi Chayim HaLevi Donen
Basic Books, 2001

The Halachos of Brochos
Rabbi Yisroel Bodner
Phillip Feldheim, Inc., 1997

6. Tzitsis

The *mitzvah* of *tzitsis* is mentioned twice in the Torah:

"...they are to make for themselves fringes on the corners of their garments throughout their generations, and to attach a thread of blue on the fringes of each corner. They shall be to you as tzitsis, and you shall look upon them and remember all the commandments of the L-rd and fulfill them, and you will not follow after your heart and after your eyes by which you go astray - so that you may remember and fulfill all My commandments and be holy to your G-d..." Bamidbar 15:38

"You shall make for yourself twisted cords upon the corners of your covering, wherewith you cover yourself." Devorim 22:12

In brief, this *mitzvah* consists of one positive and one negative principle:

a) to remind us of all the commandments so that we observe them

b) to prevent us from following our heart and eyes

This *mitzvah* also helps us to elevate ourselves to a level of sanctity and devotion to G-d. How can the sight of the *tzitsis* help us realize our spiritual side? *Tzitsis* hints to the 613 precepts of the Torah: the numerical equivalent of the word *tzitsis* is 600. In addition, there are eight threads, and five knots for a total of 613.

The five knots indicate that we must bind ourselves to the five Books of Moses, while eight threads suggest the eight organs that attract man to sin: the ears, eyes, mouth, nose, hands, feet, genitals, and the heart. *Tzitsis* remind man of his Divine obligation (the 613 precepts of the Torah) and of his need to guard against desires related to these organs.

Just like a uniform identifies a soldier, *tzitsis* are part of the uniform of a Jew. Many men wear a four-cornered wool or linen garment called a *tallis koton*, under their shirt, so they can fulfill this *mitzvah*. *Tzitsis* are also part of the large *tallis* "prayer shawl" that men put on before praying. (By the way, a prayer shawl should be made of wool and be large enough to wrap around yourself and still cover your knees.)

Before putting on your *tallis koton* place the threads in your left hand, look at them to make sure that they haven't been torn off, and say this blessing:

Boruch Atah Ado-noy Elo-hai-nu	"Blessed are You, L-rd our G-d
Me-lech Ho-Olom	King of the universe,
Asher Kiddeshanu	Who sanctified us
B'mitz-vo-sav V'tzi-vonu	with His commandments,

commanding us

Al Mitz-vas Tzitsis.   concerning the *mitzvah* of *Tzitsis.*"

During Biblical times, a blue thread (*tcheles*) was included among the white threads. According to our sages, blue resembles the color of the sea, and the sea resembles the color of the heavens, and the heavens resemble the 'color' of G-d's Throne of Glory."

Today, many people are unsure of the snail from which the blue dye was extracted. However, we can still recall its significance whenever we read the precept of *tcheles*. The word *tcheles* is related to the Hebrew word, *tachlis* "purpose." The absolute purpose and goal of everything we do should be recognition of, and attachment, to G-d.

Words of Wisdom

Looking leads to remembering, and remembering leads to doing, as it is said, "That you may remember and do." (*Vayikra* 15:40)

For Further Reading:

The Laws of Tzitzis, A practical guide.
Rabbi Aharon Pollak
Targum/Feldheim, 2002

7. Tefillin

The commandment to wear *tefillin* is found Deut. 6:8, *"You shall bind them as a sign upon your hand, and they should be for a reminder between your eyes."*

Our sages explain that *tefillin* consist of two small leather boxes with leather straps. Each box contains four Torah sections inscribed on parchment:

(1) The *Shema* (Deut. 6:4-9) - the Unity of the One G-d

(2) *Vehayah* (Deut. 11:13-21) - the concept of reward and punishment

(3) *Kadesh* (Ex. 13:1-10) - the duty to remember the redemption from Egyptian bondage

(4) *Vehayah* (Ex 13:11-16) - the obligation of every Jew to teach his children (and students)

The *mitzvah* applies to men and boys thirteen and over. The *tefillin shel yad*, "hand-*tefillin*" are worn on the biceps of the "weaker" arm. A right-handed person puts *tefillin* on his left arm. A left-handed person wears them on his right arm. In either case, the *tefillin* should rest against the heart, the seat of the emotions. The straps of the *tefillin* are wound seven times around the left arm and three times around the middle finger of that hand. We wear the *tefillin shel rosh, the* "head-*tefillin*," at the hairline above the forehead, so it rests upon the intellect.

Wearing *tefillin* on the arm opposite the heart, and on the head, teaches us that we must submit our mind, heart and actions to the Almighty. It also teaches us that the intellect must rule over the emotions. Sadly, many people let their emotions control the mind, and use their intellect to rationalize their behavior. Wearing *tefillin* helps us overcome this tendency. It also helps unite our intellect, emotion, and action, thereby devoting all our faculties to G-d.

The question can be asked, "If *tefillin* symbolizes devoting oneself entirely to G-d, shouldn't I wait until I become observant before wearing them? Isn't putting on *tefillin* before doing other *mitzvos* being hypocritical? The answer is that each *mitzvah* has its own value, and its own reward. So the fact that one does (or does not) do one *mitzvah* should not prevent the person from performing another. In addition, our sages say that the "One *mitzvah* leads to another." Eventually, the more you do and the more you learn, the more you will want to take on many *mitzvos*. In the meantime, you should wear *tefillin* even if you don't relate to it.

There's another point. G-d gave us time so that we could spiritually grow, develop, and evolve. Putting on *tefillin* or performing any other *mitzvah* should be viewed as one more step along that path, one more way we connect to our Source.

By the way, *tefillin*, like all *mitzvos*, represent the *Ratzon* (Will) of G-d. Since women are innately connected to *Ratzon*, they already have those qualities that men achieve by wearing *tefillin*.

Select Laws of Tefillin

Every aspect of *tefillin* has deep religious and *kabbalistic* significance. Therefore, you should only purchase them from a dependable source.

Tefillin are only worn on weekdays (Sunday through Friday). On Shabbos and festivals, including *chol-hamoed*, (intermediate days of a festival), we do not wear *tefillin*. (Some congregations also don *tefillin* donned on *chol-hamoed*.)

Tefillin are worn during the morning prayers. However, if for some reason it was impossible to wear them in the morning, you may don them on later in the day, but not after sunset.

The person should stand when putting on *tefillin*.

Step 1. Take the hand-*tefillin* out of its container, and position it on the biceps of the weaker arm. Adjust the *tefillin* so it is positioned close to the heart.

Step 2. Before tightening the straps, recite the following:

Baruch Atoh Ado-noi Elo-heinu	"Blessed are You, L-rd our G-d,
Melech HaOlam	King of the universe
Asher Kiddeshanu	Who has sanctified us with

| *B'mitzvosav Vitzsivanu* | His commandments, commanding us |
| *L'ho-niach Tefillin.* | to don *tefillin*." |

You should not talk or gesture while putting on *tefillin*.

If you made any type of interruption, say the following:

Baruch Atoh Ado-noi Elo-heinu	"Blessed are You, L-rd our G-d,
Melech HaOlam	King of the universe
Asher Kiddeshanu	Who has sanctified us
B'mitzvosav Vitzsivanu	with His commandments, commanding us
Al Mitzvos Tefillin.	concerning the *mitzvah* of *tefillin*."

Step 3. Tighten the strap by wrapping it twice over both the leather base of the hand-*tefillin*. You should now have three loops around your biceps, forming the shape of the letter *Shin*.

Step 4. Wrap the leather straps seven times down the length of your forearm. Wind the remaining strap around your palm.

Step 5. Place the head-*tefillin* above the forehead, and so that the knot in the back rests on the nape of the neck. Position the head-*tefillin* so that it is above the hairline and centered between the eyes. Run the two straps down your front. The black sides must face outward.

Step 6. Unwind the strap from your palm. Loop it around the middle finger, first around the lower phalanx near the palm, again around on the middle phalanx, and again around the lower phalanx. The shape should look similar to the letter *yud*.

Wind the remaining strap around the palm and loop it around so that a knot is formed. (The straps of both the hand- and head-*tefillin* must always be worn black side up.)

One should not interrupt the act of donning *tefillin*. One can say "Amen" when hearing someone else make the blessing.

The *tefillin* should be placed on the bare arm and without anything intervening.

If for some reason you cannot put the hand-*tefillin* on, you can still don the head-*tefillin*, and vice versa. In each case, say the appropriate blessing, *L'Haneach Tefillin* over the hand-*tefillin* and *Al Mitzvos Tefillin* over the head–*tefillin*.

You should be constantly and respectfully aware of the *tefillin* while wearing them.

It is customary to stand when removing the *tefillin* after morning service. On Rosh Chodesh (the first of the month), we remove them before *Musaf* (the additional service of the morning.) (Those who wear *tefillin* on *chol-hamoed*, remove them before the *Hallel* prayer).

To remove your *tefillin*, stand and unwind the strap around the middle finger and wind it around the palm. Remove the head-*tefillin* using your "weaker" hand. Store the head-*tefillin* in the *tefillin* bag. Remove the hand-*tefillin* and place it in the bag. Put the head-*teffilin* on the right and the hand-*tefillin* on the left.

When a *tallis* is worn during prayer, put it on first. Once you have finished services, remove the *tefillin* and then your prayer shawl.

On *Tisha b'Av*, the *tefillin* are not worn for the morning service, but are worn for the afternoon service.

The *tefillin* must be handled carefully. If you drop them, G-d forbid, give charity. Some men fast. (Ask your rabbi what to do.)

Prayer said while wearing tefillin

Say the *Shema*. Cover your eyes with the right hand while saying the first line of *Shema*.

She-ma Yis-ro-el	"Hear, O Israel,
Ado-noy Elo-hay-nu	the L-rd is our G-d,
Ado-noy Ech-od.	the L-rd is One."
Bo-ruch Shaym	"Blessed be the name of
Ke-vod Mal-chu-so	of His glorious Kingdom
Le-olom Vo-ed.	forever and ever."

You can find the complete *Shema* in the section on prayer.

Words of Wisdom

There is no difference between scrolls of Torah, on one hand, and *tefillin* and *mezuzos* on the other. (Genesis Rabbah)

Rav Zera's disciples asked him: How did you manage to live such a long life? He answered: In all my years, I never lost my temper in the midst of my family. I have never walked even one step before one who was greater. When I found myself in a soiled alley, I avoided meditating on Torah. I have never walked four cubits without studying Torah and without wearing *tefillin*..." (Talmud Megillah 28a)

For Further Reading:
Tefillin: The Inside Story
Rabbi Moshe Emanual
Targum Press, 1995

Tefillin
Rabbi Arye Kaplan
NCSY/ Union of Orthodox Jewish Congregations, 1986

8. Prayer

The Hebrew word for prayer, *tefila*, is related to the word, *p'lillim*, means to "judge oneself." Prayer helps us work on ourselves so that we can become better people. At the same time, our sages compare prayer to Jacob's ladder. It began on earth yet reached to the heavens. In other words, prayer enables us to attach ourselves directly to G-d.

In a brilliant essay, Rabbi Avrohom Chaim Feuer, writes,

> "Before prayer, we seem to be gripped by many forces beyond our control—history, heredity, society, competitors, nature—all conspiring to trap us in their tenacious web. After prayer there is hope. When we pray, we elevate ourselves and leave the world behind. Prayer places us in the presence of G-d, and we deal with Him directly, exclusively. In His kindness, G-d allows us to negotiate with Him, as it were. The very act of recognizing and acknowledging the Creator has made us His partners in Creation.

Where there is prayer, nothing else exists–only man and G-d. Facts and figures fall away; precedents and predictions disappear. All that matters is the plea of man and the will of G-d. Prayer is not a duel, a struggle between two opposing wills, rather it is an attempt to achieve a merger of wills. Indeed, our prayers are an opportunity to yield ourselves to His will, but by virtue of our submission to G-d, we can hope that He will grant our plea[30].

In general, our prayers fall into four groups. We praise G-d, thank G-d, confess our transgressions, and ask G-d to fulfill requests.

For a thousand years after Moses, there were no formal prayers. People either learned prayers from their elders or colleagues, or they composed their own prayers. They also prayed when and where they felt appropriate. During the times of the Tabernacle and Holy Temple, sacrifices were offered in the morning and evening, lasting into the night. Therefore, it became common for men to pray at these times.

Many of today's prayers were established by Ezra and the men of the Great Assembly around the time of the Second Temple. Over the next 800 years, the actual order and form of our prayers became fixed. These prayers were recorded in a *Siddur,* which means "order." The oldest known *siddur* is that of Rav Amram Gaon, Head of the Yeshiva of Sura in Babylon (present-day Iraq). It is about 1100 years old.

---

[30] Feuer, Rabbi Avrohom Chaim, *Shemoneh Eserai*, Mesorah Publications, Brooklyn, NY, 1999, p.15-16

Preparing for Prayer

How do we pray? The early sages used to spend an hour before prayer just getting ready. One way to prepare is to generate awe and love for G-d by concentrating on how He manifests His presence. This should be done in great detail, either from this world up to the highest spheres or from the highest spheres down to this lowly world. The idea is to realize how great G-d is and how He invests energy into all of creation, from the tiniest quark to the most massive black hole, past, present, future, all derive from Him; and there is no place devoid of Him.

Another approach is to consider one's own life; what one has done, where one is spiritually, how many years left in one's life. Once we realize how far we are from G-dliness, we will strongly desire to come close to G-d. This desire should drive our prayers. Interestingly, the effort to pray is called *avodah*, which means service through effort. In the book My Prayer, Rabbi Nissan Mindel explains,

> The plain meaning of *avodah* is "work." We work with a raw material and convert it into a refined and finished product. In the process, we remove the impurities, or roughness, of the raw material, whether it be a piece of wood or a rough diamond, and make it into a thing of usefulness or beauty. The tanner, for example, takes a raw hide and by various processes converts it into fine leather....*Tefilah* (prayer) in the sense of

avodah is the "refinery" where the impurities of character are done away with.[31]"

In addition to formal prayers, Judaism also encourages us to "talk to G-d" in our own way. This "conversation" can take place anywhere and about anything. Everything can be revealed, our hopes, fears, requests, and complaints. According to our sages, G-d desires our complete reliance on Him for all our needs, no matter how small, and so we should express ourselves often.

Perhaps the greatest example of that self-expression is *Tehillim*, which literally means "praises" but more commonly is referred to as Psalms. King David composed most of them. Moses, and even Adam, also composed Psalms. The 150 chapters of Psalms reflect virtually every emotional nuance of man. No other literature has ever come close to the beauty, power, and simplicity of psalms. It is unique, not only in its ability to express the days of our lives, but in the way Jews (and non-Jews) have adopted Psalms to express their own heartfelt needs. Perhaps the most well-known Psalm is Number 23:

A Psalm by David.

The L-rd is my shepherd. I shall lack nothing.

He makes me lie down in green pastures;

He leads me beside still waters.

He revives my soul;

He directs me in paths of righteousness for the sake of His Name.

---

[31] Mindel, Rabbi Nissan, *My Prayer*, Kehot Publishing Society, Brooklyn, New York, 1973, P. 5

Even if I will walk in the valley of the shadow of death,

I will fear no evil, for You are with me;

Your rod and Your staff – they will comfort me.

You will prepare a table for me before my enemies;

You have anointed my head with oil; my cup is full.

Only goodness and kindness shall follow me all the days of my life, and

I will dwell in the House of the L-rd for many long years[32].

The 150 chapters of Psalms are divided into five books that correspond to the five books of Moses (Torah). They can also be divided into the days of the week and month. It is customary to say the Psalm that corresponds to your age. If you are 30, you would say the 31st Psalm because it is actually your 31st year.

[32] Mangel, Rabbi Nissen, *Siddur Tehillat Hashem*, Merkos L'Inyonie Chinuch, Brooklyn, NY, 1992, p. 146

Pennies from Heaven

One time a villager came into the synagogue looking very sad.

"What's wrong Beryl?" the rabbi asked.

"I dreamed that G-d spoke to me last night," Beryl confessed.

"That's wonderful." the rabbi exclaimed.

"No it's not. You see, it says in Psalms that one day in G-d's eyes equals a thousand years, so I thought that one ruble in G-d's eyes must equal a thousand rubles. In my dream, I asked G-d for one His rubles. And He answered me."

"What was His answer?" the rabbi asked excitedly.

"He said, "Wait a day.""

Intention

Whether we are saying Psalms, praying, or performing a *mitzvah*, we should have both concentration and intention. As we mentioned earlier, this is known as *kavana*. Often, we rush into things out of habit. To a certain extent, *kavana* is the act of breaking that habit. Maimonides in his Laws of Prayer (4:16) writes, "*Kavana* means that the worshipper must clear his mind of all private thoughts and regard himself as standing before the Divine Presence. If his thoughts are wandering or occupied with other things, he should not pray. He should pray quietly and with feeling, not like one who is trying to unload a burden...."[33]

There are a couple of "tricks" that can help us overcome this challenge. One is to pause before praying and "empty your head of irrelevant thoughts." Another trick is to point to each word as you read it. Another trick is to speak the word loud enough to hear and understand.

Selection of Prayers

A father is happiest when children love and respect each other. So, too, G-d showers us with His love and kindness when we show love, respect, and kindness to our Jewish brothers and sisters.

Hareini M'kabel Alai Mitzvah Asaeh	"I take upon myself the positive command:
Shel V'ahavta L'reyecha Kamocha.	You shall love your neighbor (your fellow Jew) as yourself. "

In general, there are three dimensions to existence. There is the place, there is the time, and there is the person involved. The following prayer links all three parts with a request for G-d's bountiful blessings:

Mah Tovu Ohalecha Yaakov, Mishkanosecha Yisroel.	"How goodly are your tents, Yaakov, your dwelling places, Yisroel

---

33 Maimonides, *Hilchos Tefila,* Translated by Rabbi Eli Touger, Moznaim, 1989, P. 174

V'ani B'rov Hasdecha Avo	And I, through Your great kindness come
Beisecha Eshtachave	to Your House; I bow to
el Hachal Kadshecha B'yirasecha.	Your holy sanctuary in awe of You
V'ani Sfilasi Lcha Ado-noi	And may my prayer to you, L-rd be at
Es Ratzon	an auspicious time
Elo-him B'rov Chasdecha	G-d, in your abundant kindness
Anaini B'emet Yishecha.	Answer me with Your true salvation."

For 20 centuries, the Jewish people have prayed for the Third Holy Temple to be built, ushering in the Era of *Moshiach*. The following brief prayer expresses those 2000 years of longing:

Yehi Ratzon Milfanecha	"May it be Your will before You
Ado-noi Elo-heinu V'elohay Avoseinu	L-rd, G-d, and G-d of our fathers
She'yibane bais Hamikdash	to rebuild the Holy Temple
Bimhera Biyameinu	speedily in our days
V'san chelkeinu b'sorasecha.	and give us our portion in Your Torah."

This is one of the most lyrical prayers in the liturgy:

Adon Olam Asher Mawlach	"L-rd of the Universe Who reigned
B'terem Kol Yitzur Nivrah	Before anything was created
L'ais Naasa B'Chevzto Kol	At the time when by His Will, All things were made
Azai Melech Shmo Nikra	Then His Name was proclaimed King
V'Acharae Kichlos HaKol	And after all things will end,
Lvado Yimloch Norah	Alone, the Awesome One will continue to reign
V'hu Haya, V'hu Hoveh,	He was, He is,
V'hu Yehyeh B'Sifara	and He will be in glory
V'hu Echad V'Ain Shaini	He is One and nothing
L'Hamshil Lo L'Hachbira	Can compare to Him, to consort with Him
B'Li Raishis, B'li Sachlis	Without beginning, without end,
V'Lo HaOz V'Hamisra	Power and dominion are His
V'hu Ali V'Chai Goali	He is my G-d and my living Redeemer
V'tsur Chevli B'Aais Tzara	The rock of my lot in a time of distress
V'hu Nisi Umanos Li	He is my banner and my refuge

Mnas Cosi B'yom Ekra	My portion on the day that I call
B'yado Afkid Ruchi	Into his Hand, I entrust my spirit
B'Ais Ishan V'awira	At the time that I sleep and when I wake
V'im Ruchi Giviasi	And with my soul and body
Ado-noi Li V'Lo Eera.	G-d is with me, I shall not fear."

The following prayer introduces the portion of the morning service called "songs of praise." *Baruch SheAmar* contains the word, *boruch*, "blessed" thirteen times. It hints to G-d's 13 attributes of mercy. The number 13 is also the numerical value of the word, *echad*, meaning "One." Before saying the prayer, stand up, gather the two front *tzitsis* together, and say:

L'shaim Yichud Kudsha Brich Hu	"For the sake of the Union of the Holy One blessed Be He
U'shechintay l'yachada Sheim	with His *Shechina* (Divine Presence) to unite the Name
Yud-Hay B'Vav Hay	*Yud-Hay* with (the name) *Vav-Hay* in a perfect and
Yechuda Shlim B'shaim Kol Yisroel	complete union in the name of all Israel."

While holding the *tzitsis* together, say

Baruch ShAmar V'Haya HaOlam, Baruch Hu,	"Blessed is He who spoke, and the world was made. Blessed is He.
Baruch Omer V'Oseh	Blessed is He who says and does.
Baruch Gozer Umkayeim	Blessed is He Who decrees and fulfills.
Baruch Oseh V'Reishis	Blessed is He Who creates the universe.
Baruch M'Racheim Al HaAretz	Blessed is He Who has compassion on the earth.
Baruch M'Racheim HaBrios	Blessed is He Who has compassion on the creatures.
Baruch Mshalem Sachar Tov Lirayav,	Blessed is He Who rewards well those
Baruch Chai V'kayam Lanetzach.	who fear Him. Blessed is He Who lives and exists forever
Baruch Podeh U'Matziel, Baruch Shmo.	Blessed is He Who redeems and saves, Blessed is His name.
Baruch Atah Ado-noi Elo-heinu Melech HaOlam	Blessed are You L-rd, our G-d, King of the universe
HaEl Av HaRachaman HaMulal B'feh Amo	benevolent G-d, merciful Father, praised by the mouth of his people
M'Shubach U'Mfoar Bilshon	exalted and glorified by the

Chasidav l'Avidav U'vShirei Dovid Avdecha	tongue of His pious ones and His servants and by the songs of Dovid Your Servant
Nehalelcha Ad-noi Elo-heinu B'Shvachos u'Vzmiros	We will exalt You, L-rd our G-d with praises and songs;
N'Gadelcha U'nshabechacha, u'nfarecha V'Namlich-cha,	We will exalt, laud and glorify You, proclaim You King
V'Nazkir Shimcha Malkeinu Elo-heinu	and mention Your Name, our King, our G-d
Yachid Chay HaOlamim Melech	You are the only One – the life of the worlds, King
M'shubach U'Mfoar Aday v	praised and glorified is His great Name forever and ever
Baruch Atah Ado-Noi Melech M'Hulal Batishbachos.	Blessed are You, L-rd, King who is extolled with praises."

It is customary to kiss the ends of the two front *tzitsis upon completing the prayer*.

Shema

The *Shema* Prayer describes the relationship of the Jewish people to our Creator. In *Shema*, we proclaim the Unity of G-d, our submission and devotion to the reign of G-d, love of G-d, self-sacrifice for G-d, and our responsibility to study Torah and teach our children and students. We recite the *Shema* in every morning and evening service, then once again before retiring for the night.

Every Jew should try to say *Shema* at the time of one's passing. It is the essential creed of the Jew.

She-ma Yis-ro-el	"Hear, O Israel,
Ado-noy Elo-hay-nu	the L-rd is our G-d,
Ado-noy Ech-od.	the L-rd is One."
Bo-ruch Shaym	"Blessed be the name of
Ke-vod Mal-chu-so	of His glorious Kingdom
Le-olom Vo-ed	forever and ever."
Ve-ohavto Ays Ado-noy Elo-He-cho	"You shall love the L-rd your G-d
Bechol Levov-cha Uve-chol Naf-she-cho Uve-chol Meo-decho.	with all your heart, with all your soul, and with all your might.
Ve-ho-yu Ha-de-vorim Ho-eleh Asher Ono-chee Me-tzav-cho Ha-yom al Le-vove-cho.	And these words that I command you today shall be upon your heart.
Veshi-nan-tom Levo-ne-cha Ve-dibar-to Bom,	You shall teach them thoroughly to your children and you shall speak of them
Be-shiv-techo Be-vai-se-cho	when you dwell in your house.
Uve-lech-techo Va-derech	and when you walk on the way

uve-shoch-be-cho Uve-kume-cho.	when you lie down and when you rise.
Uke-shar-tom L'-os Al Yo-de-cho	You shall bind them as a sign upon your hand
Ve-ho-yu L'-to-to-fos Bain Eine-cha.	And they shall be for a reminder between your eyes
Uk-savtom Al Me-zuzos Beis-echo	And you shall write them upon the doorposts of your house
U-vi-shorecho.	and upon your gates."

Ve-ho-yo, Im Sho-mo-a Tish-meu El Mitz-vo-sy, Ah-sher Ono-chi m'tza-ve Es-chem Ha-yom, Le-ah-ha-vo Es Ado-noy Elo-Hay-chem Ul-ov-do Be-chol Le-vav-chem Uve-chol naf-she-chem. Ve-nasa-tee Mtar Artzechem B'ito Yoreh umalkosh, v'asafta d'ganecha, v'Siroshcha v'Yitzharecha. V'Nasati Esev B'Sadcha L'vehemtecha Ve-achalto Ve-savata. Hee-shomru lo-chem Pen Yifteh l'vav-chem, V'sartem V'avadtem Elo-heem Ah-chay-reem Ve-heesh-ta-cha-vee-sem Lahem. V'chara Ahf Ado-noy Ba-chem V'atzar Es Ha-shmayim Ve-lo YeYeh Matar v'Ha-adma lo See-tayn Es Ye-vu-lo, Va-avadtem M'hayra May-al Ha-aretz Ha-tovah-asher Ado-noy No-sayn Lo-chem. V'Samtem es divrei eleh al L'vavchem v'al nafshechem ukshartem osam l'os al Yedchem v'hayu L'totafos bein Einechem. V'lemad-tem Osom Es benaychem Le-da-bayr Bom, Be-shiv-te-cho B'vasecha. U'vlechtecha baderech u'v shachbcha uvkumecha. Uch-sav-tom Ahl Me-zu-zos Bay-se-co U-veesho-re-cho. Le-ma-an Yeer-bu Ye-may-chem V'ymay Benay-

chem Al Ho-ah-do-mo, Ah-sherNeesh-ba Ado-noy L'a vo-say-chem

L'says Lo-hem, Kee-y'may Hashmayim A Ha-aretz.

"And it will be, if you will diligently obey My commandments that I enjoin upon you this day, to love the L-rd your G-d and to serve Him with all your heart and with all your soul, I will give rain for your land at the proper time, the early rain and the late rain, and you will gather your grain, your wine, your oil. And I will give grass in your fields for your cattle, and you will eat and be sated. Take care lest your heart be lured away, and you turn astray and worship alien gods and bow down to them. For then the L-rd's wrath will flare up against you, and He will close the heavens so that there will be no rain and the earth will not yield its produce, and you will swiftly perish from the good land that the L-rd gives you. Therefore, place these words of Mine upon your heart and upon your soul, and bind them for a sign on your hand, and they should be a reminder between your eyes. You shall teach them to your children, to speak of them when you sit in your house and when you walk on the road, when you lie down, and when you rise. And you shall inscribe them on the doorposts of your house and of your gates - so that your days and the days of your children may be prolonged on the land that the L-rd swore to your fathers to give to them for as long as the heavens are above the earth."

Va-yo-mer Ado-noy El Moshe Lay-mor: Da-bayr El Be-nay Yis-ro-el Ve-amarta Alay-hem V'a su Lahem Tzitsis al Kanfe V'egdayhem Le-do-ro-som. V'nosnu Lo-hem Tzitsis ha-ko-nof, P'sil T'chay-les. Ve-ho-yo Lachem Le- Tzitsis, U'reesem O-so, Uzchar-tem, Es Kol Mitzvos Ado-noy, Va-ah-see-sem, O-som. Ve-lo Sosu-ru ahcharay L'vav-chem Ve-ahcharay Aynay-chem Ahsher Ahtem zo-neem Ahcharayhem. Le-maan tizke-ru V'a-sisem Es Kol Mitz-vo-soy, Vee-he-yee-sem kedoshim Lay-lo-hay-chem. Ah-nee Ado-noy Elo-Hay-chem, ah-sher Ho-tzay-see Es-chem, May-eretz Mitz-ray-yeem Lee-he-yos Lochem Lay-lo-heem, Ah-nee Ado-noy Elo-Hay-chem. Emes.

"And the L-rd spoke to Moses, saying: Speak to the children of Israel and tell them to make for themselves fringes on the corners of their garments throughout their generations, and to attach a thread of blue on the fringes of each corner. They shall be to you as tzitsis, and you shall look upon them and remember all the commandments of the L-rd and fulfill them, and you will not follow after your heart and after your eyes by that you go astray - so that you may remember and fulfill all My commandments and be holy to your G-d. I am the L-rd your G-d who brought you out of the land of Egypt to be your G-d; I, the L-rd, am your G-d. True."

Shemoneh Esrai

Shemoneh Esrai means "eighteen." It refers to the number of blessings that this prayer originally contained. The prayer is also known as the *Amidah* or "standing" prayer. We pray *Shemoneh Esrai* facing Jerusalem and the site of the Holy Temple. This is typically east. We also stand with our feet together, like a soldier who stands at attention before his commanding officer. We only look into the *siddur* and do not interrupt this prayer for anything.

The *Shemoneh Esrai* contains three themes. The first three blessings praise G-d. The next 13 blessings contain requests for us and the Jewish people at large. The last three blessings thank G-d and ask for His continued presence in our lives.

In *Shemoneh Esrai*, the essential Jewish soul that is a part of G-d connects and becomes nullified to its G-dly Source. We emphasize this by declaring, "My L-rd, open my lips, and my mouth shall declare Your praise" before we begin *Shemoneh Esrai*. We also emphasize our nullification by bowing at specific times during the prayer.

At first glance, it may seem strange to request give G-d a laundry list of requests during *Shemoneh Esrai*. But this is a perfect place to state our needs because our ego is not involved. Rather, we are asking for the ability to fulfill G-d's will in a physical world unhindered by obstacles.

You can find the text of the *Shemoneh Esrai* in any traditional prayer book.

Select Laws of Shemoneh Esrai
During *Shemoneh Esrai*, we bow four times.

1. When saying the first word, *Boruch*, "Blessed" we bend our knees. At the second word, *atoh*, "You" we bow our heads. At the third word, *Ado-noi*, "L-rd" we straighten.

2. We repeat this at the end of the first blessing. At *Boruch*, we bend our knees. At *atoh*, we bow forward. And at *Ado-noy*, we raise up. Then we finish the blessing by saying, *magain Avrohom*.

3. When we say the words, *Modim Anachnu Lach*, "We thankfully recognize..." we simply bow without bending the knee.

4. Before the end of *Shemoneh Esrai*, we find the blessing, *hatov shimcha lecha naeh l'hodos*, "it is fitting to offer You thanks..." At the beginning of this blessing, we bow like we did earlier. At the first word, *Boruch*, we bend our knees. At the second word, *atoh*, we bow. At the third word, *Ado-noi*, we stand straight.

During certain times of the year, we add special parts to *Shemoneh Esrai*. For example, during the 10 days between Rosh Hashana and Yom Kippur, we mention the idea of doing *teshuva* "return-repentance" before the King. On fast days, we ask G-d to forgive us and hear our cry for help. On Rosh Chodesh and the intermediate days of *Pesach* and *Sukkos* we ask G-d to accept our prayers on these special occasions. And on *Purim* and *Chanukah*, we recall the miracles that occurred.

In addition, we change certain parts of *Shemoneh Esrai* to correspond to the summer and winter season in Israel. In the summer, we say *morid hatal*, "He causes the dew to descend." In the winter we say, *mashiv haruach umorid hageshem*, "He causes the wind to blow and the rain to fall."

In the blessing of *Borech aleinu*, we also switch. In the summer we say, *v'sain brocha*, and "place your blessing" and in the winter, we switch to *vsain tal umatar l'vrocha*, "and place dew and rain for a blessing"

Shemona Esrai is so important that the one who prays at the head of the congregation repeats it with 10 men, i.e., a *minyan*, present. This way, people who do not know this prayer can also take part in it. Members of a *minyan* participate three ways:

1. Whenever we hear the name of G-d, *Ado-noi*, we say, *Boruch Hu, uboruch shmo*, "blessed his He and blessed is His name." And at the end of every blessing, we say, Amen.

2. When the leader repeats *Shemoneh Esrai*, we say *kedusha*, "praise of sanctification" at the end of the second blessing. The prophet Isaiah says the angels declare, "Holy, holy, holy is the L-rd of Hosts, the whole earth is full of His glory." The expressions, "Blessed is the glory of the L-rd from its place" and

"The L-rd shall reign forever; your G-d O Zion, throughout all the generations. Praise the L-rd." are associated with the angels. When the entire congregation stands in unison, feet together, and recite the same words, we too are like angels praising G-d.

3. When the *baal tefilah* says, *Modim*, "We acknowledge," we bow and quietly say this special prayer at the same time. One reason is that this prayer thanks G-d for the many things He does for us. We say it as well so that we don't appear to be ungrateful.

Shemona Esrai ends with *sholom*, peace. Our sages say that peace is the greatest blessing of all.

6 Remembrances

At the end of our prayers, we mention six things that Torah commanded us to recall:

1. (So that you) remember the day you came out of the land of Egypt all the days of your life.
2. But beware and carefully guard your soul lest you forget the things that your eyes have seen, and lest they be removed from your heart all the days of your life; make known to your children and to your children's children (what you saw) on the day when you stood before the L-rd your God at Chorev (Sinai).
3. Remember what Amalek did to you on the way as you came out of Egypt; how he met you on the way, and cut down all the weak who straggled behind you, when you were weary and exhausted; and he did not fear G-d. Therefore, when the L-rd your G-d will relieve you of all your enemies

around you, in the land that the L-rd your G-d gives you as a hereditary portion, you shall blot out the memory of Amalek from under heaven. Do not forget.

4. Remember, do not forget, how you provoked the L-rd your G-d to wrath in the desert.

5. Remember what the L-rd your G-d did to Miriam on the way, as you came out of Egypt.

6. Remember the Shabbos day to sanctify it.[34]

As mentioned earlier, Jews pray three services daily, corresponding to Abraham, Isaac, and Jacob. The services also correspond to offerings that were made in the Holy Temple. Daily offerings were brought every morning and afternoon, while offerings could be burned all night.

Shacharis

The morning service is the longest of the three. It follows the structure of a ladder. It begins with morning blessings followed by Psalms and sections from *Tanach* to make us more aware of the importance of G-d in our lives. We then say *Shema*, proclaiming our devotion to G-d. It is followed by *Shemoneh Esrai*, which contains our requests. After *Shemoneh Esrai*, we say extra Psalms and prayers of supplication and gratitude, and end with *Aleinu*. (This prayer was composed by Joshua, Moshe's disciple. It praises and thanks G-d for choosing us from among the nations of the world.)

---

[34] P. 86

On Shabbos, Rosh Chodesh (first of the month), and festivals, we add an extra service after the morning prayers. The *Musaf* or "additional service" corresponds to the additional offering that was brought in the Holy Temple for that particular day.

Mincha

The afternoon service consists of four prayers, *Ashrai* (Psalm 145 with a two-line introduction from Psalm 144), *Shemoneh Esrai*. *Tachanun* (prayer of forgiveness), *Aleinu*.

Maariv

The evening service consists of three prayers. Similar to the morning, we say two introductory blessings and *Shema*. We follow it with *Shemoneh Esrai*. We end the service with *Aleinu*.

Krias Shema al ha Mitah

It is customary for Jews to reflect on the day's activities, and to put "our house in order" (from a spiritual point of view) before going to sleep for the night. We do this during a service of *Krias Shema al ha Mitah*, "Reading *Shema* upon one's bed." It consists of several brief prayers. They include a statement forgiving anyone who may have angered us during the day. We say this because we do not want others to be punished for anything they may have innocently done to us. Similarly, we don't want to be punished for anything we may have done to someone else.

Krias Shema includes the complete *Shema* prayer, as well as prayers asking to be forgiven for any misdeeds and asking for our sleep to be sweet and healthy. The service ends with this blessing:

Baruch Atoh Ado-noi Elo-heinu Melech HaOlom	"Blessed are You L-rd Our G-d King of the Universe
Hamapil Chevlai Shaina Al Eieni	Who causes the bonds of sleep upon my eyes
UsNuma Al Afapai, Umair L'eshan bas eyin.	and slumber upon my eyelids, and Who gives light to the apple of the eye.
V'Yehi Ratzon Milfanecha Ado-noy Elohai Valohay Avosai	And May it be Your will L-rd my G-d and G-d of my fathers,
SheTashkivaini L'shalom	to let me lie down in peace
V'SaAmidani L'chaim Tovim U'lshalom	and raise me up to a good life and peace.
V'Al Yvahaluni Rayoni V'Halomos Rayim V'Hirhurim Rayim	Let my thoughts not trouble me, nor bad dreams, nor sinful fancies,
UsHeyi Mitasi Shlaima Lifanecha	and may my bed be perfect before You.
V'Haer Eynei Pen Ishan HaMaves	Give light to my eyes, lest I sleep that of death
Baruch Atoh Ado-noi HaMaeir L'Olam Kulo B'Chvodo	Blessed are You L-rd who in His glory gives light to the whole world."

Ideally, you should not eat, drink, or speak after saying this.

Words of Wisdom

Prayer without intention and devotion is like a body without a soul. (*Yeshuos Meshicho 14:1*)

When praying, remember before whom you are standing. (*Berachos* 28)

What great nation is there, that has G-d so near unto them, as the L-rd our G-d is whenever we call upon him?" (Devorim 4:7)

For Further Reading:

Shemoneh Eserai
Rabbi Avrohom Chaim Feuer
Mesorah Publications, 1990

My Prayer
 Rabbi Nissan Mindel
Kehot Publication Society, 1998

A Call to the Infinite
Rabbi Aryeh Kaplan
Moznaim Publishers, 1986

9. Talmud Torah

In *Devorim* (5:10), the Torah commands us to "Learn them and safeguard them so that you will be able to do them." Without learning, it's impossible to know what to do.

Therefore, our sages have said that we should learn in the morning and in the evening. The morning usually means right after prayer, as the Code of Jewish Law (27:1), states "After prayer, a person should establish a fixed time for Torah study. This session should be established and not skipped[35]...."

The *mitzvah* of learning Torah applies to every person, rich or poor, young or old. If you cannot study because you lack the knowledge or materials, you should help others who can study by donating to a yeshiva, purchasing books for them, etc.

---

[35] Ganzfried, Rabbi Shlomo, Kitzur Shulchon Oruch, translated by Rabbi E. Touger, Moznaim Publishing Corp., NY, NY, 1991, p. 124

In Chapter II, we mentioned that there are five levels of Torah, the *Pshat*, "the simple meaning," *Remez*, "allusion", *Drush*, "homilies", *Sod*, "secrets of Torah," and *Chassidus*, "path to serving G-d." Each level teaches us about living our lives in the holiest manner possible. Ideally, these levels form the steps of a ladder. A person should first learn the meaning of important texts and how we fulfill that meaning by following the laws.

For example, one of the 10 commandments is "Honor your father and mother." The Torah teaches us how to fulfill it. In the *Shulchan Aruch* (Code of Jewish Law), we learn that we honour parents by fulfilling their wishes (as long as those wishes don't contradict the Torah), by not standing in their place or sitting in their seat, by speaking to them with respect, by providing them with their needs, etc. If we look in the Talmud, we can learn just how far we should go to fulfill the *mitzvah*. For example, the Jerusalem Talmud (Peah 1) records the story of Dama ben Nethina, a non-Jew who lived in Ashkelon. He owned precious gems that could be used to decorate the coat of the *Cohain Gadol* (High Priest). The sages traveled from Jerusalem to Ashkelon and offered Dama 600 thousand golden dinars to sell the jewels but he refused. Dama kept the jewels in a safe. However, the key to the box was under his father's pillow, and at the time, his father was sleeping. Dama turned down 600,000 golden dinars rather than disturb his father. The sages bought the jewels from another source. However, G-d rewarded Dama for his act. A red heifer was born in his herd. Once again, the sages approached him. This time, Dama replied, "I know that you are prepared to pay any amount for the red heifer. However, I only want the amount that I lost when my father was asleep." He obviously received it.

Learning Torah has many other benefits besides helping us understand our religious obligations. The Torah represents Wisdom that is totally united with the Essence of G-d. When we learn Torah, we completely merge with the Creator. It's a type of unity that no other *mitzvah* can provide. That is why our sages said, *Talmud Torah kneged kulam*. Studying Torah is equal to all the *mitzvos*.

There's another advantage to studying Torah (the Wisdom of G-d): it leads to performing *mitzvos* that represent the Will of G-d. For example, it is G-d's will that we honor our parents or give charity. Learning Torah naturally leads to and enhances the way we perform *mitzvos*. Since learning Torah is also *mitzvah*, it connects us to both the Wisdom and Will of the Creator at the same time.

As a way to fulfill this *Mitzvah*, the Lubavitcher Rebbe, Rabbi M.M. Schneerson, has encouraged everyone to purchase Jewish books. Having Jewish holy books demonstrates that Jewish values are important. At the same time, their presence reminds us to use them. The more books the better. However at a minimum, we should have a *Chumash* (Five Books of Moses), a Book of Psalms, and a *siddur* (Prayer Book).

On a deeper level, our sages have taught that the world stands on three things: on the study of Torah, on the service of G-d, and on charity. Our forefathers, Abraham, Isaac, and Jacob represent these three pillars. The *Mishna* relates that the forefathers were mentioned daily in the Holy Temple to provide a measure of spiritual strength and aid in the service of G-d. Every morning, the Temple official would say, "Go out and see if the time has come to perform the morning sacrifice." If it had arrived, the lookout replied, "The whole of the east is lit up." Those below would ask, "Up to Hebron?" and he would reply, "Yes."

The commentators on the *Mishna* explain that the officials in the Holy Temple mentioned Hebron every morning to invoke the merits of Abraham, Isaac, and Jacob, who are all buried in Hebron. Similarly, having a *Chumash* (Five Books of Moses), book of Psalms, and *siddur*, recalls the merit of our forefathers, and the three pillars on which the world stands. For example, the book of Psalms (as well as a charity box) represents Abraham who served G-d through charity to men. A *siddur* represents Isaac who excelled in Prayer and a *Chumash* represent Jacob who established the tents of Torah.

Yet there is another *mitzvah* associated with the Torah. According to Maimonides, there is a *mitzvah* to write a Torah. As you may know, a Torah is hand-written on parchment by a specially trained scribe. It contains 304,805 letters. If just one letter is not written properly, the entire Torah is not kosher. To fulfill the *mitzvah* of writing a Torah, it is the custom to purchase a letter in a Torah. Interestingly, the merit of buying a letter in a Torah is alluded to in the book of Daniel:

"There shall be a time of trouble such as there never was since there was a nation until that time. And that time your people shall be delivered, everyone who shall be found written in the book." (Daniel, 12:1)

Your local Orthodox Rabbi can help you perform this *mitzvah*.

Words of Wisdom

The study of Torah is equivalent to all [the *mitzvos*]. (Kiddushin 40b)

G-d created the *yetzer hara* (selfish drive), but also the Torah as its antidote. (*Kiddushin* 30a)

The world stands on three things: Torah, worship, and good deeds. (*Avos* 1:2)

For Further Reading:

Mishnayos (Series)
Rabbi Pinchas Kehati
World Zionist Organization, 2005

The Midrash Says
Rabbi M. Weissman
Benei Yaakov Publications, 1980

The Talmud (Series)
Mesorah Publishers, 1992

10. Mezuzah

It is the custom of a king's palace to have guards at every gate. The guards serve two functions: they publicize the importance of the location, and protect the contents and individuals within.

From a Jewish perspective, attaching parchment scrolls called *mezuzos* to the doorpost of practically every room serves the same purpose. They proclaim that the house is devoted to Jewish ideals. At the same time, they protect the contents and individuals both inside and out of the house.

The *mezuzah* actually refers to a parchment scroll that contains the two Biblical passages that mention this Divine commandment (*Devorim* 6:4-9 and 11:13-21), "and you write them upon the doorpost of your house and upon your gates." The scroll is inscribed in the same manner and using the same script as a Torah. The outside of the *mezuzah* contains the Divine name *Sha-dai*. In addition to being one of the names of G-d, it is an acronym of three Hebrew words that mean: "Guardian of the doorways (homes) of Israel."

Sandy A. was expecting her second child. But instead of feeling happy and excited, Sandy felt weak. At first, she thought that it was morning sickness and that soon it would go away. When she didn't feel any better, Sandy visited her doctor. He said that she was losing weight and strength. If she didn't improve, he would have to hospitalize her for several months.

With her permission, some friends asked the Lubavitcher Rebbe for a blessing. He responded, "Check your *mezuzos*." But Sandy refused. Her father lived in Israel and had recently sent her 11 *mezuzos* for her new home. "They're from Israel. They must be kosher," she explained.

Meanwhile, Sandy continued losing weight. Again, the doctor warned her. But she simply could not keep food down and was becoming too weak to even try. In desperation, she agreed to have a qualified Rabbi check all 11 *mezuzos*. Nine were not kosher. She replaced her *mezuzos* and slowly her health returned. At the end of nine months, she gave birth to a healthy full term baby boy.

Over the years, the Rebbe has made a point of encouraging people to check their *mezuzos* as a way to help improve their health, livelihood, or personal relationships. What is the connection between health, etc. and *mezuzos*?

In Chapter 2, we defined *Toras Chaim* as the "Torah of Life." But *Toras Chaim* also means "Living Torah." The Torah is woven into the three dimensions of creation: time, place, and soul. By Divine Providence, Torah portions will be read on specific days, and will contain lessons that will apply to those who are reading them. If there is a flaw in a letter of the Torah, G-d forbid, it is not there "by accident." It contains a message to all those who are present.

For example, the great scholar from 16th century Portugal, Rabbi Yitzchok Abuhav, wrote a Torah that was used regularly in his synagogue in Safed, Israel. One *Shabbos*, there was a debate over a particular word. Some members of the congregation read the word one way. Others read it a completely different way. Neither group could see how the other could make such a mistake. Upon closer examination, the Rabbi found that all the men who had purified themselves in a *mikvah* (ritual immersion pool) that morning read the word according to tradition. Those who had skipped the *mikvah* saw a totally different word. Ever since then, the Rabbis of the Abuhav Synagogue only read the Torah on Rosh Hashana, Yom Kippur, and Shavuous, when they are confident that all the men have visited the *mikvah*.

Since *mezuzos* (and *tefillin*) are written in the same manner as a Torah, they have a similar sanctity and sensitivity to Divine Providence and will reflect the spiritual energies of those around them. Therefore, it's a custom to check these articles to make sure that the spiritual channels for blessings are open. Due to their sanctity and their ability to reflect the spiritual energies, many people will only buy *mezuzos* and *tefillin* from reliable sources.

Select Laws Concerning a Mezuzah

1. Homes, offices, public buildings, even the gates to private courtyard, even the gates to a city require *mezuzos*.

2. All doors of the house, including those leading to corridors, porches, fire escapes, etc. should have a *mezuzah*.

3. Some places do not require a *mezuzah*, e.g., a prison, a *mikvah*, or a synagogue. In addition, *mezuzos* should not be affixed in inappropriate places, e.g., the entrance to toilets, bathrooms, showers, locker rooms, etc.

4. No additions should be made to the text of the *mezuzah*.

5. Outside the Holy Land, the duty of affixing a *mezuzah* in a rented apartment begins on the 30th day after moving in.

6. The *mezuzah* is folded so that "*Shema*"- which is on the right-hand side of the written page, should be on the top, with the writing inside starting from left to right.

7. Before being affixed, place the *mezuzah* in a protective cover or case. It could be made of glass, wood, metal, or any other material.

8. The *mezuzah* should have its upper part pointing forward, at that angle, towards the entrance of the room.

9. It should be placed over 2/3rds of the way up the doorpost.

10. Before affixing a *mezuzah* (or many *mezuzos*) say the following blessing:

Boruch Atah Ado-noy Elo-hai-nu lech Ho-Olom	"Blessed are You, L-rd our G-d, King of the universe
Asher Kid-shonu B'mitz-vo-sov	Who has sanctified us with His commandments,
V'tzi-vonu	And commanded us
Likboa Mezuzah.	concerning the affixing of the *mezuzah*."

It is a custom to check *mezuzos* (and *tefillin*) at least twice every seven years. Many people have the custom to check them more often. (Unfortunately, printed, improperly written, and otherwise unsatisfactory *mezuzos* have flooded the public market. In addition, many *mezuzos* that were originally proper have since faded or cracked due to age or weather. A competent authority should periodically check all one's *mezuzos*.)

For information concerning where to acquire kosher *mezuzos*, where to have your present *mezuzos* examined, which doors require *mezuzah*, etc., contact your local Orthodox rabbi.

Words of Wisdom

Ardavan sent an exquisite pearl to the great sage Rav and asked, "Send me something of equal value in return." Rav gave him a *mezuzah*. Ardavan sent back a message, "I gave you something beyond value and you sent me something that you can purchase for a coin." Rav replied, "Neither my possessions nor yours can match it [for true value.] You sent me something that I must guard, whereas I sent you something that guards you while you sleep, as Proverbs 6:22 states, "When you walk, it shall lead you; when you lie down it shall guard you."

For Further Reading:

The World of Tefillin and Mezuzos
Rabbi Zeev Rothschild,
STAM Publications

11. Kashrus

In *Vayikra* 11:9, the Torah presents the signs of kosher animals, birds, fish, and insects, and permits or prohibits various species of animals. The Torah also has many other laws that deal with eating, such as not to eat the sinew of the thigh, not to mix milk and meat, etc. All dietary laws fall in the category of *kashrus*. *Kosher* means "fit" or "proper."

The laws of keeping kosher are *chukim*, statutes, meaning a decree from G-d.[36] Nevertheless, our Rabbis have found many reasons for the laws of *kashrus*. One of the most famous has become a common saying: "We are what we eat." This adage recognizes that food spiritually affects the one who consumes it. If something is not kosher, it's incompatible with our soul.

Spiritual incompatibility is one explanation for the laws of *kashrut*. Yet researchers have found many health benefits, as

---

36 As mentioned earlier, *Chukim* are G-dly decrees that are beyond logic.

well. For example, pig meat may have trichinosis. Eating milk and meat together is hard to digest. However these explanations are side issues, for no matter how healthy or unhealthy a particular item is, its kosher status represents the Will of G-d. Therefore, *kashrus* is not a set of laws that can become outdated through modern methods of sanitation, food inspection, or production[37].

In general, food falls into three categories, milk, meat, and *pareve* (neither milk nor meat).

Meat

Any meat or fowl, and/or food made with meat and fowl products like bones, soup or gravy are *fleishig* (meat). Similarly, meat ingredients in any product (including liver pills), must meet *all* requirements for kosher meat. Among them:

1. The animal chews its cud and has split hooves.

2. It must be slaughtered according to Jewish law by a skilled and carefully trained kosher *shochet*, "ritually trained slaughterer."

3. The permissible animal parts must be salted before cooking.

---

[37] For example, Jewish law states that we must use milk from a kosher animal. To ensure that the milk is from a kosher animal or hasn't been mixed with the milk of a non-kosher animal, a Jew must be present during its processing. (Milk and milk products supervised by a Jew from the time of milking through their complete processing are known as *Cholov Yisroel*, "Jewish milk.") Today, government inspection allows us to be reasonably certain of the source of various milk products. Still, the law does not change. If you have a problem keeping *Cholov Yisrael* due to health, unavailability, etc., ask a Rav what to do. There is another point. Many people feel that if the packaging does not contain non-kosher ingredients, the item must be kosher. According to the government, ingredients used in small quantities do not have to be listed. Also food processors can change ingredients yet continue using their old labels until new labels are printed. So you cannot rely on government regulations to determine the kashrus of a product.

There are many laws concerning the kashrus of meat.

Bladerunner

The knife used to slaughter an animal is called a *chalaf*. The blade must be surgically sharp. The tiniest nick causes the knife and the meat to be *trafe* (literally "torn,"), meaning "non-kosher." To make sure that the blade is perfectly smooth, the shochet will run his fingernail across the blade, feeling for imperfections.

As a freelance writer, I once attended a meeting about a new product. It was a "smoothness tester." At the time, it was the most advanced instrument of its type on the market and could gauge surface imperfections down to .0001 of an inch. During the presentation the engineer casually mentioned that, while the company's instrument could measure the depth of any imperfections, the human fingernail was just as accurate in finding them.

Dairy

The term *milchig*, "dairy" refers to all types of milk, butter, cream and yogurt, and every variety of cheese, whether hard or soft. It also refers to milk derivatives such as sodium caseinate and lactose. Even the smallest amount of dairy in a food causes the food to become dairy. Therefore, you should not eat or use these foods with meat products.

Dairy foods require certification verifying that the milk and cheeses:

1. Are from a kosher animal.

2. Have no meat-fats or any meat substances mixed into them.

3. Contain no non-kosher substances.

Pareve

Foods that are not meat or dairy, or their derivatives, are considered *pareve* "neutral." *Pareve* foods can generally be served with either meat or dairy meals, can be prepared in meat or dairy pots, and may be served on meat or dairy dishes. However, *pareve* foods cooked in a meat pot may be only served on meat dishes. Similarly, *pareve* foods cooked in dairy pots may be served only in dairy dishes.

Pareve food cooked with meat or dairy products become "*fleishig*" or "*milchig*" respectively. If the *pareve* foods only touched milk or meat, you can wash it and the food will remain *pareve*, as long as a) the *pareve* and meat or milk items are room temperature or cooler, b) and all the items have not been mixed with pungent or sharp foods such as onions, lemons, pickles, etc.

It is not necessary to have a separate set of dishes for *pareve* foods. However, it is common to set aside serving trays and especially bakeware as *pareve*. These are always washed separately from meat and dairy dishes. You should also have separate dish sponges, dish towels, draining boards, etc. Below are some laws pertaining to *pareve* foods.

Fish

To be kosher, fish must have both *fins* and *scales*.

Eggs

Eggs must be opened and examined. A blood spot in an egg, whether raw, cooked, or fried, renders that egg unkosher. Each egg should be opened into a glass examined before being cooked or mixed with other eggs. If you find a blood spot, the whole egg should be discarded and the vessel washed in cold water. According to Jewish tradition, it is advisable to cook at least three eggs at a time.

Leafy Vegetables and Grains

Green leafy vegetables and certain grains and fruits that could contain worms and insects must be inspected before they can be used. You should examine these foods thoroughly and even wash them in cold water to remove any worm or insect. An insect does not, however, make the food or utensil non-kosher. You can simply remove it. It is also common to find worms in packages of noodles, etc., especially if they have been stored for a long time.

Oil

In recipes where oil or shortening is required, it must be pure vegetable shortening, as many oils contain animal fats. To ensure that the oil being used is free of animal fats, it must be under strict Rabbinic supervision.

Basic *Pareve* Foods

Following is a list of some *pareve* foods. They are *pareve* as long as they do not contain any meat or dairy products. Products that have been processed must have reliable supervision.

Breads*	Soft drinks	Juices
Some cakes grains	Eggs	All
Some hard candy vegetables	All types of kosher fish	All
Cereals*	All fruits	Cookies*

*An increasing number of food processors are adding milk products to obtain extra Vitamin D and calcium. For example, candy and cereal often contain milk products, as do some low-calorie sweeteners. Often, commercial *kashrus* organizations will publish bulletins describing changes in the condition of items, labeling mistakes, or other vital information. To make sure that the items that you're buying are kosher, you should visit their sites on the Internet or subscribe to their publications.

Separating Meat and Dairy

The prohibition against combining meat and dairy foods is mentioned in the Torah, elaborated in the Talmud, and passed down through the generations of the Prophets and Rabbis. It teaches us that this prohibition applies three different ways.

1. Eating: We must not eat any meat and dairy foods or their derivatives together.
2. Cooking: We must not cook any meat and dairy foods together. The term cooking includes baking, frying, roasting, etc.
3. Benefiting: Not to have any benefit from meat and dairy foods cooked together such as selling or doing business with such foods.

To avoid any transgression, it's customary to have two sets of dishes, silverware, and cleaning utensils.

Here are some rules about separating meat and dairy foods:

You shouldn't have meat and dairy foods at the same meal even if they were made separately and even if you wait between eating.

After eating dairy, you should rinse your mouth and eat something *pareve*, ideally with a hard consistency. Most people wait one-half hour after eating dairy before they will eat meat or meat products. Other people wait one hour. Certain hard cheeses (Swiss, Muenster, etc.) stick to your teeth and take longer to digest. These require waiting *six-hours* before eating meat.

If you eat meat, you must wait *six full hours* before eating dairy. If you find a small piece of meat between your teeth after six hours, you should remove it and rinse your mouth. However, you do not have to wait another six hours.

If you are on a special diet and for children under nine years old, you should consult a *Rav*. If there are no special problems, you should train children early to wait between eating meat and dairy.

The six-hour waiting period is standard for all Jews, except those groups that have *halachically* established other customs.

If you do not chew or swallow the food, but spit it immediately from your mouth, you don't have to wait. You should still rinse your mouth well. However, if you have chewed or swallowed even the smallest amount of food, you have to wait.

If *pareve* foods were prepared in meat or dairy utensils that were not used within the last twenty-four hours, then even though that item may not be eaten with the opposite type of food, the waiting period is not necessary.

However, if the *pareve* food is sharp or spicy, then even if the utensils were not used with hot meat or dairy respectively within the last 24 hours, they may not be eaten with the opposite food.

Concerning the waiting period for these, and the definition of the terms sharp, spicy, and hot, consult a qualified rabbi.

The Deeper Meaning of Kashrus.

"For I am the L-rd your G-d; sanctify yourself therefore and be holy; for I am holy." (Vayikra 11:44)

The passage mentions holiness and sanctification yet it is found in the Torah section dealing with *kashrus*. To understand how spiritual terms such as holiness and sanctification relate to such physical activities such as eating, we should look to another verse. This one is in *Devorim* (8:3), "Man does not live by bread alone, but by every word that proceeds out of the mouth of the L-rd does man live."

Kabbalah and *Chassidus* explain that the "G-dly spark" in the food is the true source of nourishment for man. It enables man to benefit from something that is on a spiritually lower level. At the same time, man is able to elevate this spark of the physical, thereby making this world a fit dwelling place for G-d. In return, the individual becomes spiritually refined and better able to receive G-d's blessings.

From a slightly different perspective, our sages teach us that each Jewish home is compared to a "miniature, personal Holy Temple," i.e., a dwelling place for the Divine Presence. The table in the home is compared to the Altar. In the Sanctuary, only perfect offerings were brought upon the altar and consumed. Similarly, we should only consume food that is absolutely proper for serving the Creator.

Words of Wisdom

You are what you eat. (Common folk saying)

Eat according to your means. (Genesis Rabbah)

Two Chassidim were comparing the greatness of their respective Rebbes. "My Rebbe can heal the sick." the first Chassid proclaimed, and then he asked, "What can your Rebbe do that makes him so special? "My Rebbe?" exclaimed the other Chassid. "Why, he can eat without bending his head down to his food. Instead, he "elevates" his food up to his head."

For Further Reading:

Going Kosher in 30 Days
Rabbi Zalmen Goldstein
The Jewish Learning Group, 2007

Spice and Spirit of Kosher Cooking
Kehot Publication Society, 2002

Meat and Dairy
Ehud Rosenberg
Feldheim, 2004

To be a Jew
Chaim Donen
Basic Books, 1991

12. Tzedokah

Often, *Tzedokah* is translated as "charity." But its true meaning is "righteousness." The less fortunate deserve help and the Torah commands us to provide it.

The *mitzvah* to help those in need (typically, the poor) is found twice in the Torah. *Vayikra* 25:35 states, "And if your brother becomes poor and cannot maintain himself then you shall assist him, both the stranger and/or sojourner (in order) that he live with you."

The *mitzvah* is also found in *Devorim*, 15:7-10, "If there be among you a needy man, any one of your brethren within any of your gates in the land that the L-rd your G-d gives you; you shall not harden your heart, nor shut your hand in the face of your needy brother. But you shall open wide your hand to him, and shall surely lend him sufficient for his need...."

Interestingly, the Hebrew word meaning "to give" is *nosain*. It is spelled the same way backwards and forwards. According to our sages, this teaches us that the one who gives also receives.

Abraham was the first person to donate 10% of his wealth to *tzedokah*. This is one reason that Maimonides writes (Hilchos Matanos Aniyim 10:1), "We must be careful to fulfill the *mitzvah* of *tzedokah* more than any of the other positive commandments, for *tzedokah* is a sign of a righteous person, the trademark of Abraham's children…"

Maimonides lists eight levels of *tzedakah*, starting from the highest and most praiseworthy:

1. Helping a person find work or learn a trade
2. Giving secretly to someone you don't know
3. Giving secretly to someone you do know
4. The giver doesn't know who received, but the receiver knows who gave
5. Giving before you were asked
6. Giving after you were asked
7. Giving, but not as much as you can afford
8. Giving against your will

The Torah provides a number of different ways to give *tzedokah*. They include providing food or clothing to the poor, helping a needy bride and groom, and offering hospitality to strangers. If you don't have money, you can give *tzedokah* spiritually by helping others learn about their Jewish heritage. According to

Rabbi Levi (*Vayikra Rabba* 24), "If you don't have anything to give him, comfort him at least with consoling words."

The Talmud (Bava Batra 9) states that *tzedokah* outweighs all other commandments. It is so great that it is called "the *mitzvah*."

It is customary to give *tzedokah* every day except *Shabbos* and holidays. It is a custom for all Jews to give before praying and for girls to give before lighting *Shabbos* and *yom tov* candles.

What makes the *mitzvah* of *tzedokah* so special? In general, people are intensely involved in earning money. Not only that, they use most of their money for necessities, such as food, clothing, etc. Taking money that they could have used and giving it to others is an act of self-sacrifice.

On a deeper level, Rabbi Shneur Zalman, the first Rebbe of Chabad said (Tanya, Igeres Hakodesh CH.21), "the effect and mystical consequence is to elicit and draw down supernal life from the Fountainhead of Life...[*tzedokah* has this effect] because the arousal [that man initiates] from below to revive the spirit of the humble "who has nothing at all of his own," elicits an arousal from Above[38].

No wonder our sages say that, "Great is *tzedokah*, for it brings the Redemption closer. (Bava Basra 10a)"

---

[38] Lessons in Tanya, Volume 5, Kehot Publication Society, New York, New York, 1997, P, 9, 11

13. Ahavas Yisroel

Vayikra 19:18, the Torah commands us 'You shall love your fellow like yourself.' This is the *mitzvah* of *Ahavas Yisroel*, "love of a fellow Jew." According to Rabbi Akiva, it represents a cardinal principle of the Torah.

Kabbalah and *Chassidus* explain that the souls of Jewish people are a "portion" of G-d, their Creator. This means that the souls of all Jews share the same source. Therefore, the commandment "love your fellow Jew as yourself" can be taken literally, because your fellow Jew is part of yourself. In fact, our sages have said that the Jewish people make up one spiritual body. The rabbis serve as the "eyes" of the congregation. Those who are involved with the needs of the community are the "hands." Those who financially support Torah scholars are called the "legs."

The point is, the Jewish people are truly one. Every person is important and no person is more important than any other. Nine Moses' could not form a *minyan*. Ten Jews who may not have learned Hebrew can. In fact, our sages say that the Divine Presence hovers over 10 Jews without exception.

In *Judaism: Thought and Legend*, Rabbi Meir Meiseles writes,

> "What lies at the root of peace, happiness and everything which is good and beautiful in the world? The invariable answer would be love. Not a superabundance of sentiment gushing out upon everyone, nor ostentatious philanthropy, but a simple, impartial, warm feeling of kinship with everyone, irrespective of person and place, a feeling which is nurtured on the knowledge that everyone is a living soul, that everyone resembles ourselves and is our natural brother.[39]"

Our sages taught that the Holy Temple in Jerusalem was destroyed because people hated each other without reason. Showing love, sensitivity, and respect to others above and beyond reason can help rebuild it, speedily in our days.

Acts of Kindness

Gemilas Chassadim means acts of loving kindness. The Torah states, "After the L-rd your G-d shall you walk...and unto Him shall you cleave." (Deut. 13:5). Our rabbis wonder how it is possible for a human being to copy the Divine Presence?"

They answer that the commandment to "walk after the L-rd your G-d" means to mimic His attributes and ways. For example, as G-d is called merciful and gracious, so should you be merciful and gracious. As G-d clothed Adam and Eve who were naked, so should you clothe those in need. As G-d visited Abraham after he

---

[39] Judaism Thought and Legend; Meiseles, Rabbi Meir, Feldheim, Jerusalem, 1977, p. 14

was circumcised, so should you visit the sick. As G-d comforted Isaac over the passing of Sarah, so should you comfort mourners.

On the surface, the *mitzvah* of *Gemilas Chassadim* is similar to *tzedokah*. However, *tzedakah* typically refers to helping the less fortunate with their physical and spiritual needs. The *mitzvah* of performing acts of kindness applies to the poor and the rich, to the living and for those who passed on, to those who deserve and those who do not. And while the Rabbis set limits to the amount of money we should give to *tzedokah* (so that we shouldn't become poor), there's no limit to the acts of kindness that we could, or should, perform.

What acts qualify as *gemilas chassadim*? In general, the *mitzvah* covers any kind of personal service that we perform for another. Typically these include:

- Loaning money or any an object without charging a fee or interest
- Providing hospitality
- Visiting and comforting the sick
- Soothing those in need
- Helping a bride and groom
- Burying the dead
- Comforting mourners
- Restoring peace between husband and wife, employer and employee, neighbor and friend

Our sages claim that the world stands on three things: *Torah*, *Avodah* (prayer), and *Gemilas Chassadim*. The Talmud and

Jewish history are filled with many examples of people who excelled in this *mitzvah*. For example, the *Gemara* (*Yerushalmi, Shekalim* 5.4) writes that a blind person once visited the home of Rabbi Eliezer ben Jacob. Rabbi Eliezer placed the blind man at the head of his table, while he sat among his other guests. Those guests naturally assumed that the blind man was an important person. As a result, they gave him gifts and large donations so that he could live without worry. They were shocked when the blind man asked, "Why do you honor me so much?" They replied, "If Rabbi Eliezer ben Jacob sits below you at his table, should we not honor you, as well?" The blind man then told Rabbi Eliezer the following, "You have performed an act of kindness for one who is seen but cannot see; therefore, you will be blessed by Him Who sees, yet cannot be seen."

Rabbi Shneur Zalman of Liadi was a master of both the revealed and mystical parts of the Torah and Rebbe of many Chassidim. On Yom Kippur, Rabbi Shneur Zalman led the prayers of the congregation. However soon after the services began on one particular Yom Kippur, Rabbi Shneur Zalman left the synagogue and disappeared into the night. After a while, he returned and continued to lead the congregation. Later, the community found out what had happened. A young wife had just given birth and her husband had gone to the *shul*. She and her newborn were alone, and once the candles and fire had gone out, the house had become quite dark and cold. In his holiness, Rabbi Zalman heard her "cries" for help. So he, stopped his petitions before G-d, left the synagogue, and visited the poor and lonely mother and her child. There, he arranged a fire and prepared something warm for the mother. Only then did he return to the services.

According to our sages, G-d prefers kind deeds more than the sacrifices that were offered in the Holy Temple, as Hosea writes (6.6) "For acts of kindness I desired and not sacrifice."

Words of Wisdom

Rabbi Israel Baal Shem Tov, the founder of Chassidism, states that "The love of Israel is the love of G-d, as the Torah (Deut.14:1) says, 'You are children of the L-rd your G-d.' And when one loves the Father, one loves the children."

14. Teshuva

Teshuva means "return." It is the ability to renew our relationship with G-d after we have jeopardized it. In a sense, *teshuva* is greater than Torah because it enables us to overcome the spiritual damage that we caused by transgressing G-d's commandments. Once, a great Rabbi asked his disciples, "How far is it from East to West?" The students struggled to come up with an answer that would satisfy their understanding of the question, but they failed. Seeing their frustration, the Rabbi said, "It is not very far at all. All you have to do is turn around." Similarly, *teshuva* is the process of turning around. Yet contrary to popular belief, *teshuva* has nothing to do with afflicting oneself. Rather, it concerns changing our attitude and behavior. In the words of Maimonides, (The Laws of *Teshuva*, 1:1)

"If a person transgresses any of the mitzvos of the Torah, whether a positive command or a negative command, whether willingly or unintentionally, when he repents and turns away from his sin, he must confess before G-d, Blessed be He, as [*Bamidbar* 5:6-7] states, "If a man or a woman sins against one's fellow man...they must confess the sin that they committed." This refers to a verbal confession. This confession is a positive command."

What is complete *teshuva*? A person who confronts the same situation in which he sinned, when he has the potential to commit the sin, yet abstains and does not commit it because of his *teshuva* alone and not because of fear or a lack of strength...."(2:1)

What constitutes *teshuva*? That a sinner should abandon his sins and remove them from his thoughts, resolving in his heart, never to commit them again as [Isaiah 55:7] states, "May the wicked abandon his ways..." Similarly, he must regret the past as [Jeremiah 31:180 states, "After I returned, I regretted." [One must reach the level where] He who knows the hidden will testify concerning him that he will never return to this sin again.... (2:2)

In addition to the "3Rs" of regret, recite, and resolve, there's another act: rectify/restore. If possible, a person should try to repair whatever damage was done, both materially and spiritually. For example, if a person took something, he or she should return it to its owner. If the owner isn't known, the person should give the equivalent value to charity. Similarly, if a person wronged another by speech, he should seek to set the record straight with those who heard him. He should also ask the person who was wronged for forgiveness.

The process of *teshuva* should also drive the person to better himself, especially in those areas of weakness. For example, if a person was dishonest in some way, he or she should look for opportunities to make society a better place by promoting honesty in one's relationship with others, in the home, and in the workplace[40]. Our sages said that a person should continually do *teshuva* until one's misdeeds can be accounted like *mitzvos* because they were the cause of so much good.

In fact, Jewish law states that if a person betrothes a girl "on the condition that I am a *tzaddik*, one who is completely righteous," the betrothal is valid and she would need a bill of divorce to marry another. The reason is that *teshuva* can change the person's level (and legal status) in an instant.

To put it another way, a *tzaddik* increases in matters of holiness step by step, in an orderly fashion. But *teshuva* is so powerful that it can empower a person to leap ahead and continue moving in leaps and bounds.[41]

On a mystical level, *Kabbalah* and *Chassidus* explain that *teshuva* is composed of the two words *tashuv hey*. This means to "return the lower hey" of G-d's encompassing name composed of four letters *Yud Hey Vav Hey*. The lower *Hey* refers to *Malchus*, the *sefira* (manifestation) of Kingship. This *sefira* is also called *Shechina*, meaning the Divine Presence. When a person transgresses the laws of the King, the act forces the Divine Presence into concealment. The process of *teshuva* reunites the lower Hey with the three remaining letters of the Divine Name and leads to the revelation of G-dliness.

---

[40] Your rabbi can help you proceed down the path of *teshuva*.

[41] For most people, though, *teshuva* requires practice and time. In the beginning, you'll take two steps forward and one step back. But eventually, determination and focus can get you where you want to go. The key is to remember that observant Judaism is a process, not a destination.

On another level, *teshuva* is the process of serving G-d by returning to one's Source. This type of *teshuva* applies whether we have transgressed or not. Viewed from this perspective, every day represents a new opportunity to elevate one's garments of thought, speech, and deed. This means that even people who are perfectly righteous must do *teshuva*.

Traditionally, *teshuva* is linked to the days of Elul, the month before *Rosh Hashana* (New Year) and the ten days between *Rosh Hashana* and Yom Kippur, the Day of Atonement. During this period, we work on correcting our behavior, our relationship with our fellow men, and our relationship with G-d, so that on Yom Kippur our sins can be forgiven.

Words of Wisdom

Rend your heart, not your garments. (*Yoel* 2:13)

For Further Reading:

Overcoming Folly - Kuntres Umayaon
Rabbi Sholom Ber Schneerson
Chassidic Heritage Series, 2006

The Knowing Heart
Rabbi Moshe Chaim Luzzatto
Feldheim Publishers, 2003

The Way of G-d
Rabbi Moshe Chaim Luzzatto
Feldheim, 1981

15. Shabbos

"And G-d rested on the seventh day... and He blessed it and made it holy." (Genesis 2:3)

"Remember the Shabbos day, to keep it holy. Six days shall you labor and do all your work; but the seventh day is a Sabbath unto the L-rd you G-d; in it you shall do no type of work, neither you, your son, daughter, servant, maid-servant, cattle, nor the stranger within your gates; for in six days, the L-rd made the heaven and the earth, the sea and all that exists within, and rested on the seventh day, therefore, the L-rd blessed the Sabbath day and hallowed it." (Shemos 20: 8-11)

Shabbos is one of the greatest gifts ever given to the Jewish people. It is indeed a day of rest. But it's more than that. *Shabbos* is a day of rejuvenation, physically, mentally, and emotionally. It is an island of sanity and serenity in the sea of confusion called life. Above all, it is a reflection of the Time to Come, when mankind will be liberated from our selfish nature.

Shabbos serves as a sign that G-d created the world in six days and rested on the seventh. *Shabbos* also serves as a sign that G-d chose the Jewish people at Mount Sinai, and charged us to be "a kingdom of priests and a holy nation."

The two dimensions of *Shabbos* are hinted by two words. The first word is *zachor*, as the10 Commandments in *Shemos* 20:8, states, "Remember the Shabbos day to sanctify it." The second word is *shamor*, "to guard." In *Devorim* 5:12, the Torah states, "Guard the *Shabbos* to sanctify it." According to our sages, G-d communicated both words at the same time to the Jewish people at Mount Sinai[42].

On *Shabbos*, each Jew receives an additional soul. This "*Shabbos* soul" bestows an extra measure of light, understanding, peace, energy, strength, and last but not least, appetite. Our "*Shabbos* soul" gives us extra strength and power to reveal the Divine energy that is latent in the world.

How do we fulfill the commandment to "Remember the *Shabbos* to sanctify it?" According to our sages, we leave the world with its worries behind. We accomplish this by lighting *Shabbos* candles, dressing in different clothes, reciting *kiddush* over wine or grape juice, and eating special foods such as *challah*, special bread.

---

[42] Like *shamor* and *zachor* are associated with *Shabbos*, G-d commanded Adam, the first man two *mitzvos* to *l'avda* "work it" and *l'shamra* "to guard it." These correspond to the two commandments that G-d said directly to the Jewish people on Mount Sinai: "I am the L-rd your G-d" and "You shall have no other deities before Me." According to our sages, "I am the L-rd..." includes all the 248 positive *mitzvos* and "You shall have no other deities..." corresponds to the negative *mitzvos*.

In addition to acts that emphasize the specialness (i.e., holiness) of *Shabbos*, we avoid weekday activities, like discussing business, playing strenuous sports, and watching television or radio. In fact, we avoid all types of creative labor, even thought they may be fun, "therapeutic." etc. *Shabbos* is a time to "let go and let G-d." Our "job" is to relax and enjoy the day by *oneg*, the pleasure that comes from good food, nice clothes, good friends, even an afternoon nap. Saturday evening, we can enter the world again.

"It's G-d's Problem."

On *Shabbos*, we have to view that all our work is done, whether or not it actually is. One of the most dramatic examples of this occurred in December 1999. Back then, most software used two digits to describe the year. This worked well up through 1999. Once the calendar turned to Jan. 1st, 2000, however, people feared that the computers would switch to 1900, causing chaos. Experts predicted that banks would lose track of deposits and accounts. The navigation systems on large oil tankers would quit. The software that kept planes flying could have bugs.

At the time, my neighbor worked as a senior programmer for Westinghouse. His division built atomic-powered, electric generating plants, such as the one at Three Mile Island in Pennsylvania. To operate these plants, they generated millions of lines of code and virtually all of that code used the two-digit scheme for recording dates. Needless to say, the team developing the software patch had worked long hours. But even they didn't know whether the patch would work. As the day approached, I asked my neighbor what he thought might happen.

"I don't know," he replied honestly. "But I'm not going to worry about it."

"Why not?" I responded incredulously.

He looked at me and smiled. "Because January 1st is *Shabbos*. So it's G-d's problem, not mine."

Lighting Shabbos Candles

When G-d formed the world, He said, "Let there be light." The Lubavitcher Rebbe asked a logical question, "Why was light created first when there was no one around to benefit?" The Rebbe explains that light wasn't the first act of creation. Rather, it was its *purpose* and *goal*. Like an architect who sketches the finished building before illustrating the details, G-d said, "Let there be light." In other words, the goal is to bathe the entire world in the light of G-dliness. Through the *mitzvah* of lighting *Shabbos* (and *yom tov*) candles, G-d gave women the merit to help achieve this goal throughout the year.

From a historical perspective, our sages say that the candles lit by our matriarch Sarah lasted from one *Shabbos* to the next. After she passed away, the same miracle occurred with Isaac's bride, Rivkah. According to our sages, Rivkah began lighting the *Shabbos* lamp from the age of three.

Today, the woman of the home is responsible for lighting candles[43]. Through this pure and simple act, she changes the

---

[43] A young man who lives alone lights his own *Shabbos* candle.

atmosphere of her house from the mundane to the holy. At the same time, she officially welcomes the *Shabbos* queen into the home and helps kindle the Divine spark in every Jewish being.

In addition to married women, girls three and over are encouraged to light their own candles as a part of their education. The young girl should light before her mother.

It is customary to put a few coins into a *tzedakah pushka* (charity box) before lighting the candles. The proper time to light *Shabbos* candles is 18 minutes before sunset Friday. Young girls should light before this time.

Traditionally, women light two *Shabbos* candles, corresponding to the words, *shamor* (observe) and *zachor* (remember). Some married women add a candle for each child, recognizing that every individual brings his or her unique light into the world.

Procedure for lighting Shabbos candles

1. Light the candles.

2. Spread your hands out around the candles.

3. Draw your hands inward in a circular motion three times to accept *Shabbos*.

4. Cover your eyes with your hands and say the blessing:

Boruch Atoh Adonoi Eloheinu Melech HaOlam	"Blessed are You L-rd Our G-d King of the Universe

Asher Kideshanu Bemitzvosav	Who sanctified us with His commandments
Vitzivonu Lehadlik Ner Shel	Commanding us to light the lamp of
Shabbos Kodesh.	the holy *Shabbos*."

Bask in the glory of *Shabbos*. The time of lighting candles is especially favorable Above. Many women add their own prayers to G-d, asking for health and happiness. Their prayers are readily accepted because they are said while lighting the *Shabbos* candles.

CAUTION: The candles must be lit before sunset. It is forbidden to light candles after sunset.

Holiday Candles

In addition to lighting candles in honor of *Shabbos*, we light them to honor festivals using the following blessings:

Rosh Hashanah:

Boruch Atoh Adonoi Eloheinu Melech HaOlam	"Blessed are You L-rd Our G-d King of the Universe
Asher Kideshanu Bemitzvosav	Who sanctified us with His commandments
Vitzivonu Lehadlik Ner Shel	Commanding us to light the lamp of
Yom Hazikaron.	the Day of Rememberance."

Yom Kippur:

Boruch Atoh Adonoi Eloheinu Melech HaOlam	"Blessed are You L-rd Our G-d King of the Universe
Asher Kideshanu Bemitzvosav	Who sanctified us with His commandments
Vitzivonu Lehadlik Ner	Commanding us to light the lamp of
Shel Yom Hakipurim.	the Day of Atonement."

Shavuos, Pesach, and Succos:

Boruch Atoh Adonoi Eloheinu Melech HaOlam	"Blessed are You L-rd Our G-d King of the Universe
Asher Kideshanu Bemitzvosav	Who sanctified us with His commandments
Vitzivonu Lehadlik Ner Shel	Commanding us to light the lamp of
Yom Tov.	the Festive Day."

On the First Night of All Festivals and Lighting Candles:

Boruch Atoh Adonoi El oheinu Melech HaOlam	"Blessed are You L-rd Our G-d King of the Universe
Shehecheyonu V'kiyemonu	Who has granted us life, sustained us
Vehegeonu Lizman Hazeh	and allowed us to reach this occasion."

When Shabbos falls on a yom tov (holiday):

Boruch Atoh Adonoi Eloheinu Melech HaOlam	"Blessed are You L-rd Our G-d King of the Universe
Asher Kideshanu Bemitzvosav	Who sanctified us with His commandments

Vitzivonu Lehadlik Ner Shel	Commanding us to light the lamp of
Shabbos v'Yom Tov.	*Shabbos* and the Festive Day."

CAUTION: On *yom tov*, it is permissible to transfer fire from one flame to another. Use a pre-existing flame to light *Shabbos* or yom tov candles.

The *Midrash Yalkut Shimoni* (*Behalosicha*) states, "*If you will observe the kindling of the Shabbos lights, you will merit to see the lights of the redemption of the Jewish people.*" In the merit of the righteous women who have lit candles over the centuries, may we see the Redemption immediately.

Kabbalos Shabbos

Before the Friday evening service that ushers in *Shabbos*, we recite several Psalms and hymns. This service is called *Kabbolos Shabbos*, "welcoming *Shabbos*." Our sages compare *Shabbos* to both a queen and a bride. Just as a welcoming committee always greets the queen whenever she visits, so too, we welcome the *Shabbos* queen every week through psalms and hymns. The most famous of these prayers is *L'Cha Dodi*, "Come my beloved," by Rabbi Shlomo Alkabetz of Sfas. Having "officially" welcomed the bride, we begin *maariv*, the evening service.

Kiddush

Shabbos and holiday meals begin with *kiddush*. It is a prayer that contains blessings over wine and mentions the holiness of the special day (e.g., *Shabbos* or yom tov). The head of the house or any male over thirteen can recite *kiddush* for those present. In some homes, all males recite their own *kiddush*. The *kiddush* cup should hold four ounces of liquid. The one who recites *kiddush* drinks at least two ounces and distributes wine to the rest of the household. On Friday evening, the family members and guests stand while the *kiddush* is being recited. On Saturday afternoon, standing is a matter of custom. Everybody answers *Amen* at the end of the blessing over the wine and at the end of the blessing over the special day. The Friday night *kiddush* testifies that G-d created the world and rested on the seventh day. The afternoon *kiddush* speaks about *Shabbos* as a sign between us and G-d.

Special Meals

On *Shabbos* and *yom tov,* it is a *mitzvah* to eat one festive meal in the evening and another the following afternoon. (When *yom tov* occurs on two consecutive days, we have evening and afternoon meals both days.) The *Shabbos* and *yom tov* meals begin when the head of the household makes *kiddush* on wine.

Afterwards, everyone washes for bread. To wash for bread, fill the container. Lift it up in your left hand and pour water over your right hand up to the wrist. Repeat this twice. Then, switch the container to the right hand, wash the left hand three times. After drying your hands, say:

Baruch Atoh Ado-noi Elo-heinu	"Blessed are You, L-rd our G-d,
Melech HaOlam	King of the universe
Asher Kiddeshanu	Who has sanctified us

B'mitzvosav Vitzvivanu Al	with His commandments, commanding us
Natilas Yadaim.	to wash our hands."

After the family members and guests gather around the table, the head of the house lightly draws the knife across the *challah* to indicate the place of cutting, then raises the *challahs,* and recites the blessing, *Boruch atah...hamotzei lechem min haaretz.* Everyone responds *Amen.* He cuts a piece of *challah* for himself, dips the piece in salt, and eats it immediately. He then distributes *challah* to all those present. Each one eats a piece before speaking. A popular custom is to offer each male two small loaves of *challah* so that he may make his own blessing.

Traditionally, *challah* is served on *Shabbos, yom tov* or other special occasions. *Challah* is associated with one of the positive *mitzvos* given to women: separating *challah* dough.

When the Jewish people were about to enter the Land of Israel, G-d commanded them to give a portion of their dough to the *cohainim* (priestly tribe). Since the destruction of the Holy Temple in 70 C.E., we have been unable to perform this *mitzvah.* However, as a reminder of the past and in anticipation of the future Holy Temple, our sages have ordained that the Jewish people continue to separate a measure of dough.

The commandment to separate *challah* is found in *Bamidbar* 15:21-30. The Torah states, "Separate the first portion of your kneading as a dough offering...." This *mitzvah* symbolizes that all our sustenance comes through G-d. It also teaches us that just as we separated and offered the first of our dough to G-d, so should we separate a portion of our earnings for *tzedakah*.

The following instructions on separating *challah* come from the *Spice and Spirit Cookbook* (Kehot Publication Society):

Challah is separated while the dough is still whole, before it has been divided and shaped into loaves. Before the piece of dough is separated, say the following blessing:

Baruch Atoh Ado-noi Elo-heinu	"Blessed are You, L-rd our G-d,
Melech HaOlam	King of the universe
Asher Kiddeshanu	Who has sanctified us
B'mitzvosav Vitzvivanu	with His commandments, commanding us
L'Hafrish Challah.	to separate challah."

Remove a small piece, approximately one ounce from the dough. Immediately after separating *challah*, say "*Harai zeh challah.*" "This is challah."

Today, we cannot give the *challah* to the *cohainim* and we should not use it for ourselves. Therefore, the custom is to burn this piece separately, (e.g., in a piece of aluminum foil.) It should be burned in the oven (preferably in the broiler.) However, if one burns the *challah* in an oven, no other food should be inside.

NOTE: Although separating *challah* is one of the three mitzvos given especially to women, anyone over bar or bat mitzvah may also separate *challah*, if necessary. If you are kneading more than 3 lbs. 11 ounces of dough, you should say the blessing. If you are mixing or kneading 2 lbs. 11 ounces up to 3 lbs. 10 ounces, you should separate dough without saying a blessing. If you are mixing or kneading 2 lbs. 10 ounces or less, you do not need to say a blessing or separate *challah*.

Separating dough, like lighting candles and following the laws of *mikvah*, has a profound meaning. Just as the wonderful smell of freshly baked *challah* fills the room and envelops everyone, so too should the spirituality emanating from the world of *Kether* be revealed to those in this world. Perhaps this is linked to the sages' statement that observing the *mitzvah* of *hafrashas challah* will bring a blessing on the house.

There are many different ways to prepare *challah*. There are water *challahs*, *challahs* with poppy seeds, *challahs* with raisins, onion *challahs*, whole-wheat and honey *challahs*, water *challas*, and much more. Here is one tasty recipe from the *Spice and Spirit* cookbook:

You need:

2 ounces of fresh yeast or 4 packages of dry yeast

3.5 cups of warm water

.75 cup of sugar

1.5 tablespoons of salt

13 – 14 cups of flour

6 eggs, slightly beaten

1 cup of oil

Glaze

1 egg, beaten

poppy or sesame seeds

Use baking sheets or loaf pans

Yields 4 – 6 loaves

Instructions

1. Dissolve yeast in warm water in a large bowl. When dissolved, add sugar, salt, and half of the flour. Mix well.

2. Add eggs and oil, slowly stir in most of the remaining flour. The dough will become very thick. (Until the kneading stage, the dough can be mixed in an electric mixer.)

3. When dough begins to pull away from the sides of the bowl, turn onto floured board and knead for about 10 minutes. Add only enough flour to make dough manageable. Knead until dough is smooth and elastic and springs back when pressed lightly with the fingertip.

4. Place dough in a large oiled bowl. Turn it so the top is oiled as well. Cover with a damp towel and let rise in a warm place for 2 hours, punching down in four or five places every 20 minutes.

5. Separate *challah* with a blessing. Divide the dough into four to six parts and shape into loaves; place in well-greased bread pans or on greased baking sheet, let rise until double in bulk.

6. Preheat oven to 375°

7. Brush tops of loaves with beaten egg and sprinkle with poppy or sesame seeds. Bake for 30 to 45 minutes or until browned. Remove from pans and cool on racks[44].

8. Make a blessing....*ha motzi lechem min ha aretz* and enjoy.·

A traditional *Shabbos* or *yom tov* meal includes wine, fish and meat or chicken, as well as many other delicacies. It also includes songs, words of Torah, and stories of our sages. After the meal, everyone recites the blessings after the meal, in keeping with the Torah commandment, "When you have eaten and are satisfied you shall bless G-d your G-d" (*Devorim* 8:10). The Talmud records that Moses developed the first blessing, Joshua formulated the second, and Kings David and Solomon formulated the third. Our rabbis were responsible for the rest.

Maintaining a Shabbos Atmosphere

On *Shabbos* and *yom tov*, it is the custom to wear special clothes. During the times of the Talmud, many people didn't have special clothes for *Shabbos* or *yom tov*. Some would roll their cloaks up during the week, and unroll them for *Shabbos* or *yom tov*. Today, many people have a special suit, tie, or jacket that they only wear on these occasions.

---

[44] Spice and Spirit Cookbook, Lubavitch Women's Organization, NY, p. 50-51

On *Shabbos* and *yom tov*, it is also the custom to attend services at the synagogue and to listen to the Torah reading during the morning. The Torah is also read on *Shabbos* afternoon.

The point is that *Shabbos* is a time for "rejewvenation." During *Shabbos*, we avoid listening to the radio, watching television, or reading non-Jewish newspapers or magazines. Instead, we combine spiritual pursuits like learning with great food and fine clothes. It's the best of both worlds.

Shalosh Seudos

On *Shabbos*, it is a *mitzvah* to eat *seudos hashelishis,* "the third meal." According to the *Talmud* (*Shabbos* 118A), a person who enjoys three meals on *Shabbos* will have a good judgment in the World to Come. Some people eat bread. Others have cake or fruit. It is also the custom to sing songs and share words of Torah.

Seudas hashelishis must begin before sunset. If it is a meal with bread, it may continue until after dark. As long as the meal continues, it remains *Shabbos* for those participating, even if three stars have come out and it is night. *Shabbos* is over when those having *shalosh seudos* have said the grace after a meal, and prayed the evening service.

Havdolah

After *Shabbos* ends, we say *havdalah*, "partition" to separate the holy day of *Shabbos* and the rest of the week. You shouldn't do any work or eat any food before *havdalah*. However, if you have to do work after *Shabbos*, but before *havdalah*, you can rely on the special words we say in the evening *Shemoneh Esrai* prayer on Saturday night. (See your prayer book for details.) You can also say "*Boruch hamvdil bain kodesh l'chol,*" ("Blessed is the One Who separates between the holy and the mundane.")

Ideally, you should say *havdalah* over a cup of wine. You can also use grape juice or beer instead of wine. Havdalah also includes a blessing over spices. Why spices? Now that *Shabbos* is over and our extra spiritual soul has departed, we need a "lift." Smelling spices provides that boost.

In addition to spices, we say a blessing over a special *havdalah* candle, one that has two wicks. (If you don't have a *havdalah* candle, you can unite the flames of two candles). After the blessing, we hold our fingernails to the light to see the difference between light and dark reflected on our hands. The last blessing is *havdalah* ("Blessed art Thou, L-rd our G-d King of the Universe, who makes a distinction between the holy and the ordinary").

If you forgot to say *havdalah* Saturday night, you can say it anytime until Tuesday sunset. In this case, say a blessing on wine and *havdalah*, but not the blessings on spices and fire.

Havdalah for Yom Tov

We also say *havdalah* at the end of *yom tov*.

If *yom tov* ends Sunday through Thursday, we do not say the blessings over fire and spices. If *yom tov* ends on Friday night, we do not say *havdalah* since the holiness of *Shabbos* is greater than that of *yom tov*.

If *yom tov* <u>starts</u> Saturday night, we do not make a separate *havdalah* prayer. However, we refer to *havdalah* in the *yom tov* evening Kiddush, saying, "Blessed art Thou, L-rd our G-d King of the Universe, who makes a distinction between the holy (i.e., *Shabbos*) and the *holy* (i.e., *yom tov*)."

We make the blessing for fire on the *yom tov* candles, not a separate *havdalah* candle. However, we do not make the blessing over spices since the holiness and joy of Yom Tom make up for the departure of our *Shabbos* soul.

Melave Malka

Just as we welcomed the *Shabbos* queen with a special service, *Kabbalas Shabbos*, we accompany her out with a special meal called, *melave malka*, "escorting the queen." The Talmud relates that we receive many rewards and benefits from having a *melave malka*. The Talmud also explains that food eaten for *melave malka* nourishes the *luz* bone. This small bone is located on the top of the spine. Our sages say that it never decays and that G-d will use it to resurrect us in the days of Messiah.

Some people make a point of eating bread for *melave malka*. If bread is not available, you can have cake, cookies, or fruit. Whatever you eat, have in mind the *mitzvah* of *melave malka*.

Traditionally, we mention the name of Eliyahu HaNavi (Elijah the Prophet) on Saturday night, since he will introduce *Moshiach*. Also, he is responsible for recording the fact that we kept the *mitzvah* of *Shabbos*. We also share words of Torah.

In addition, Chassidim customarily tell stories about the Baal Shem Tov (the founder of Chassidus (1698-1760) or other great

Rabbis and *tzaddikim*. These stories help strengthen our faith and trust in G-d and our spiritual leaders.

In addition to the *mitzvah* of "Remembering the *Shabbos*, we have the *mitzvah* of *shamor*, "Guarding the *Shabbos*."

Shamor refers to guarding the day, and the uniqueness of the Jewish people, by avoiding any work. It affirms our belief that G-d truly provides our livelihood and sustenance. All the good of the past week is elevated on *Shabbos*. Simultaneously, *Shabbos* is the source of all the blessings of the week to come.

Forbidden Labor on Shabbos

The Torah forbids work. But work isn't the same as effort. In the Jewish legal sense, "work" refers to the 39 general categories of creative activity (*melacha*) used to build the *Mishkan* (portable Sanctuary that the Jews carried in the desert). These *melachos* (types of work) include weaving, dying, building, etc. (You'll find a complete list in the back of the book.) By ceasing such "creative work" one day a week, we relinquish our control over environment and remind ourselves that G-d is the Creator of all.

Laws of Cooking for Shabbos

One of the key ways that we keep *Shabbos* special is by preparing food beforehand. Here are select laws for cooking and *Shabbos*.

1. In general, all food preparations for *Shabbos* must be completed before *Shabbos*.

2. This means that the food should be at least 1/3 cooked (so that it's edible) before *Shabbos* begins. To keep food warm on

Shabbos, place it on a covered flame[45] before *Shabbos*, and remove it to serve.

3. You can only return food to the *blech* on *Shabbos* if all of the following conditions are met:

    a. The pot was lifted from the *blech* with the intention of returning it.

    b. The food is fully cooked.

    c. The food is still slightly warm.

    d. The contents were not transferred to a direct pot.

    e. The pot was not put down (on table, chair, or the like).

Note: One should keep all above in mind if you lift a teakettle off the *blech*, and intend to put it back.

4. If on *Shabbos* you see that the food is drying out, you cannot add water to it (since that water will become cooked on *Shabbos*). If you take water from a boiling kettle on the *blech*, some authorities permit it. But you should move the pot to a place on the *blech* that is not directly over the fire (providing the food is completely cooked).

5. You should not serve any food directly from a pot resting on the *blech*. You must lift the pot off.

6. To prepare a salad on *Shabbos*.

---

45 The flame and controls are covered by tin or aluminum sheet called a "blech" in Yiddish. Put the *blech* on before *Shabbos* and it keep it on the stove top until the Shabbos ends.

a. slice vegetables close to mealtime

b. when preparing the dressing, first add the oil and vinegar then salt.

Important Note: There are many more laws involved in preparing food *on Shabbos*. You should study these laws before trying to prepare everything yourself.

Our sages compare *Shabbos* to many things, including the World to Come and an island in time. One of the most unexpected yet insightful is "a ravenous wolf." What connection does *Shabbos* have to a wolf? A wolf, when cornered, will turn on its pursuers. Similarly, *Shabbos* "takes" from both Friday afternoon and Saturday night. In other words, you can't just walk into *Shabbos*. You need to prepare for it, mentally by leaving work and the weekday behind, and physically by cleaning the house, preparing food, lighting candles, etc. After *Shabbos*, it's time to wash the dishes and get ready for the week ahead. The sad news is that *Shabbos* is over. The good news is that in seven days, it will be back again.

16. The Jewish Calendar

The Jewish year is like a symphony. It is rich with themes and harmonies, dramatic highs and lows. For example, Rosh Hashana (New Year) and (Yom Kippur) are called the "Days of Awe" and the "High Holidays" to reflect their exalted status.

The Months of the Jewish Calendar:

Hebrew Month	Time frame
Tishrei	September – October
Cheshvan	October – November
Kislev	November – December
Teves	December – January
Shvat	January – February
Adar	February – March
Nissan	March – April
Iyar	April – May

Sivan	May – June
Tammuz	June – July
Av	July – August
Elul	August – Early Sept.

Pesach (Passover), *Shavuos* (Feast of Weeks), and *Succos* (Feast of Tabernacles) are called the *Shalosh Regalim*, the three Pilgrimage Festivals. During these occasions, Jewish males were obligated to appear in Jerusalem and bring sacrifices in the Holy Temple. These three holidays recall significant events in the Jewish history. *Pesach* celebrates the birth of the Jewish nation with their liberation from Egypt. *Shavuos* celebrates the giving of the Torah on Mount Sinai. *Succos* recalls the booths that housed the Jewish people on their way to the Promised Land.

The Rabbinic holidays of *Chanukah* and *Purim* celebrate victories over the physical and spiritual enemies of Judaism. We also have "minor" holidays such as *Tu b'Shvat*, the "new year for trees" and *Pesach Sheni*, "a second Passover" opportunity.

According to *Kabbalah* and *Chassidus*, these holidays not only celebrate the past, they reintroduce the Divine energy and powers that were first revealed many years ago. Every year, Passover liberates us from various forces that constrict us. *Shavuos* becomes our opportunity to receive the Torah. *Chanukah* connects us to the menorah's flame that would not go out. When observant Jews talk about time, they often put it in relation to the holidays. "*Purim* is coming." "Only six weeks to *Pesach*." "*Rosh*

Hashana is in the air." Every holiday is unique. Together, they reflect the natural patterns that exist in the life of a Jew.

Rosh Chodesh

Rosh Chodesh means the "head" of the month. The Torah commands us to celebrate the birth of the new moon and new month by offering extra sacrifices in the Temple. According to the lunar cycle, some months will have 29 days, while others will have 30 days.

During biblical times, witnesses would travel to the Great Court in Jerusalem and testify that they saw the new moon. The sages would "sanctify" the moon by proclaiming that a particular day was *Rosh Chodesh*. The sages would then send representatives to spread the word. Some outlying communities wouldn't receive the news until the 15th of the month, so they began observing two days of *Rosh Chodesh*. The 30th day of the "old" month became the first day of *Rosh Chodesh*. The first of the "new" month became the second day of *Rosh Chodesh*.

During the times of the Temple and Tabernacle in the desert, the Jews brought additional sacrifices on *Rosh Chodesh*. Today, we recite the additional service of *Musaf*. The *Shemoneh Esrai* prayer in this service contains 12 requests for blessings corresponding to the 12 months of the year.

Hillel II established the dates for Jews everywhere when he set the calendar 1600 years ago. However, we continue to keep one or two days of *Rosh Chodesh* to maintain the tradition of our ancestors. When *Moshiach* comes, we will again fix *Rosh Chodesh* by sight and proclaim it in Jerusalem.

On a deeper level, *Rosh Chodesh* is linked to the Jewish people. Every month, the moon grows larger and wanes, only to reappear and grow again over the next month. So too, the fortunes of the Jewish people follow the same path. During certain eras, the Jewish people experience both physical and spiritual prosperity. During other times, the opposite occurs (G-d forbid). This wax and wane of the moon parallel the mystical concept of *ratzo v' shov*, "advance and retreat." All things, including, the angels have this quality. They move toward their source, only to move (or be moved) back temporarily. Similarly, when a person starts becoming observant, he or she typically takes three steps forward, then two steps back, two steps forward, and one step back. It can be very frustrating. Yet *Chassidus* explains that the step backward is not a step back at all. The time of darkness, whether it is related to the new moon or to the Jewish people, serves as a preparation for even greater light.

Elul

The new year starts on *Rosh Hashana*, the first of Tishrei. But entering a new year, just like entering *Shabbos*, requires preparation. Our sages say that the month of Elul offers that time of preparation.

Rabbi Schneur Zalman of Liadi describes the role of Elul using the following parable: A king resided in a great palace all year. All year, those who wished to see him traveled great distances to the palace. Even then, they had a difficult time seeing the king. They had to make appointments with his secretaries. They had to dress appropriately. They had to learn the protocol of the court.

Once a year, the king would leave his palace and travel throughout his kingdom. At that time, he would receive everyone graciously, without regard to their appearance or palace formalities. According to Rabbi Shneur Zalman, G-d, the King of kings, is "in the field" during Elul, and at this time, He encourages us to seek Him and request His aid.

To help us make the most of this unique opportunity, we spend the month performing acts of *teshuva* "return," *tefilah* "prayer," and *tzedokah* "righteous charity." For example, during Elul, we listen to the *shofar* every morning after services (except on Shabbos and the day before Rosh Hashanah). This reminds us to "wake up from the vanities" of this world. We add Psalm 27 to our daily prayers. We say *selichos*, special prayers of praise, pardon, and forgiveness. We also give as much *tzedokah* as possible. These activities have the power to nullify any harsh judgments (G-d forbid) and enable us to enjoy a year of good.

Before *Rosh Hashana*, we say a special prayer, *Hatoras Nedorim,* *"nullification of vows"* so that we can begin the Day of Judgment without anxiety over promises that we made to G-d but did not keep. It is said in *shul* before a "rabbinic court" of least three men. *Hatoras Nedorim* does not include vows that involve others, such as a promise to repay a debt—unless they approve.

Starting in Elul, it's the custom to wish everyone *L'Shana Tova Sikatave VesachoSamie*, "You should be inscribed and sealed (in the Book of Life) for a good year."

Tishrei

Rosh Hashana

Rosh Hashana means the "Head of the Year" and stands at the pinnacle of both the past and the future. From one perspective, *Rosh Hashana* is the Day of Judgment, not only for the Jews, but also for every man, woman, and child on earth. On this day, Adam the first man was created and judged and on this day, ever since, G-d reviews our thought, speech, and deed over the last year. For that reason, *Rosh Hashana* also is a time for reflection and taking stock.

At the same time, *Rosh Hashana* is a time to look forward by making sincere resolutions for the future. This is one reason the holiday is called "the Head of the Year." *Rosh Hashana* incorporates and directs the activities of the year similar to the way that the brain directs the various faculties of a person.

Although *Rosh Hashana* is an awesome day, it is not a day for sadness. We have faith in G-d's mercy and are confident that the new year will be better than the old.

According to *Kabbala* and *Chassidus*, *Rosh Hashana* is a time when we "crown" G-d as our king. We do this by reciting special prayers throughout the holiday and by hearing the *shofar*, "rams horn." The ram's horn recalls several great milestones in our history, including the binding of Isaac on the altar on Mt. Moriah, the giving of the Torah at Mt. Sinai which was accompanied by a ram's horn, and the sound of the "great *shofar*" that will proclaim the coming of *Moshiach*, the "True Messiah."

In addition to special prayers and the *shofar*, *Rosh Hashana* has a number of unique customs. After the evening services on the first night of Rosh Hashana, we greet each other by saying, "*L'shona Tova Sikosaiv V'saicho Saim*," ("May you be inscribed and sealed (in the Book of Life) for a good year.")

To start the holiday meal at the first and second nights of *Rosh Hashanah*, we dip an apple into honey and ask G-d for a *shana tova umesuka*, a "good and sweet year." We also dip *challah* into honey and eat various sweet foods for the same reason.

On the first day of *Rosh Hashanah*, after the afternoon services, we symbolically "cast" our transgressions into a body of fresh water with live fish. This custom is known as *tashlich*, from the statement (Michah 7:19): "And you shall cast away (*tashlich*) all your sins..." If the first day of *Rosh Hashanah* falls on *Shabbos*, we say *tashlich* on the next day.

Ten Days of Repentance and Return

Rosh Hashanah, Yom Kippur, and the days between are known as the Ten Days of *Teshuvah* (repentance or return). During these days, we emphasize the mitzvos of *teshuvah, tefilah* and *tzedakah* (see Elul). The seven days between Rosh Hashanah and Yom Kippur contain the first complete week of the new year. During this special week, we can also rectify all the Sundays, Mondays, etc. of the past year.

The day after *Rosh Hashanah* is the Fast of Gedalia. It recalls the assassination of the governor of Israel after the destruction of the First Temple by the Babylonians. This fast day helps further our desire to reconnect to G-d so that G-d will reveal His special relationship to us by rebuilding the third Holy Temple.

The *Shabbos* between *Rosh Hashanah* and *Yom Kippur* is known as *Shabbos Shuva* or *Teshuva*, "the Shabbos of Return." Rabbis customarily speak to their congregations about the importance of *teshuvah* on this day. In addition, the reading of the prophets (Hosea 4:1) begins, "Return Israel unto G-d."

One custom that is mentioned in Jewish law and has support in *Kabbalah* is *kaparos* (atonement). Men and women take a rooster or hen, respectively, and say a short prayer while holding it over their heads. The rooster or hen is ritually slaughtered before our eyes (if possible) to remind us of the fate that we may well deserve for our transgressions. We then give the rooster or hen or its value to *tzedokah* to help nullify any harsh decrees. *Kaparos* can also be observed with money instead of a live chicken. The money is also held aloft and the prayer said, substituting, "This money will go to charity" for "This fowl will go to die." Afterwards, the money goes to *tzedokah*.

Yom Kippur

Yom Kippur is the Day of Atonement. It is a time when we can "erase the slate" and begin anew. *Yom Kippur* atones for misdeeds between man and his Creator. It does not atone for misdeeds between man and his fellow man unless forgiveness is granted by his fellow man. Therefore, it's the custom before *Yom*

Kippur to ask friends, relatives acquaintances, community members, business associates, etc., to forgive any wrong (whether accidental or otherwise) that may have occurred during the year. The idea, as mentioned in the Alter Rebbe's Shuchan Aruch, is that once we are forgiven by our fellow men, we are able to receive greater levels of G-d's forgiveness.

Yom Kippur lasts 25 hours, going into the 26th hour. This corresponds to the numerical equivalent of the transcendent name of G-d spelled, *Yud, Hei, Vav,* and *Hei* and pronounced, *Ado-noi.*

It is a *mitzvah* to eat two full festive meals on the day before *Yom Kippur*. It is so important that our sages say that it is equal to the *mitzvah* of fasting on *Yom Kippur* itself. Enjoying a festival meal at this time demonstrates our faith in G-d's mercy and our confidence in being sealed for a good year. It is traditional to eat *kreplach*, pieces of dough stuffed with meat or chicken, to symbolize our hope that G-d's mercy and kindness will "cover" His strict judgment. From a practical perspective, it's a "*mitzvah*" to eat lots of complex carbohydrates. They can help you get through the fast without feeling weak or terribly hungry. (Also, if possible, stop taking coffee, cola, or any other caffeine drink a few days before the fast, so that your system won't crave it.)

On the eve of *Yom Kippur*, men immerse in a *mikvah* (a pool containing no less than 200 gallons of water). The *mikvah* helps one spiritually prepare for Yom Kippur. Interestingly, the Hebrew word for "immersion," *tevilah*, has the same letters as the Hebrew word *habitul*, "nullification." This teaches us that the way to spiritual purity is by nullifying one's ego. For that reason, *Yom Kippur* is an especially auspicious time to refocus on G-d, instead of ourselves.

Five activities are forbidden on *Yom Kippur*: eating, drinking, anointing oneself with perfumes or oils, washing (for pleasure), wearing leather shoes, and marital relations. In the synagogue, many men wear a white robe called *kittel*, and women often dress in light colors or white to symbolize purity.

Every weekday, we pray in the morning, afternoon, and evening. On *Shabbos* and yom tov, we add a fourth service, *Musaf*, after the morning prayers. On *Yom Kippur*, there are five services, evening, morning, additional, afternoon, and early evening (sunset) service. These correspond to the five levels of the Jewish soul, *nefesh, ruach, neshoma, chaya, and yechida.*

The fifth prayer of the *Yom Kippur* is called *Neilah* "locking." At this time, the Jewish people stand before our Creator, symbolically with the door "locked" behind us to keep out improper worldly influences. The *neilah* service corresponds to *yechida*, the level of the soul that is united with the Creator. The doors to the Holy Ark are opened and the Jewish nation stands pouring out its collective heart before G-d. In these final moments, we have one last opportunity to utilize all the spiritual energy of the day. Using every ounce of our strength, we pray with special concentration. We end this service proclaiming our allegiance to G-d with a heart-felt "*Shema Yisroel.*" The *shofar* is then blown for the final time this year. *Yom Kippur* is an intensely and immensely powerful way to reconnect to G-d. Even though *Yom Kippur* concludes the 10 days of *teshuvah*, the spiritual process of teshuva continues throughout the year.

After *Neilah*, we say the evening weekday services, recite the *havdalah* to officially mark the separation between the holiday and the weekday, and break the fast. That night or early the next morning, it's customary to start building the *succah*, so that we can continue our spiritual climb from strength to strength.

Between *Yom Kippur* and *Succos*, there are four days, corresponding to the four letter name of G-d that is spelled *Yud Hei Vav* and *Hei*. We use this time to prepare for the holiday of *Succos*.

Succos

Succos means "booths." The holiday commemorates the booths that the Jewish people lived in during their years in the desert According to our sages, it also hints to the Clouds of Glory that surrounded and protected the Jewish people as they traveled through the desert. The Clouds of Glory reminded the Jewish people of G-d's kindness and love for His children. During *Succos*, we leave our homes and dwell in temporary booths to make us aware of and grateful for G-d's protection.

Succos has several names. The Torah calls *Succos* called *Hag Ha'asif*, "the Festival of Ingathering" because it occurs during harvest time. Our sages called the holiday the "the Season of our Rejoicing" because the Torah commands us to "rejoice" more during *Succos* than during any other holiday.

The *mitzvah* of dwelling in a *succah* is unique in several ways. It is the only *mitzvah*, other than *mikvah*, that totally surrounds one's body[46]. It is also unique in that everyone fits, i.e., is "equal," in the *succah*. Also, every time you visit, or as long as you stay in the *succah* and remember that this *mitzvah* commemorates our deliverance from Egypt, you perform a *mitzvah*. (Most *mitzvos* can only be performed once a day or for a brief amount of time.)

Selected Laws of the Succah

1. The *succah* must be built before the holiday begins.

2. A *succah* must have at least three walls. The *succah* should be large enough to contain most of a person's body.

2. You can use almost anything for the walls, but the roof covering must be made of plants that have been detached from the ground and that will last through the festival. Most people use evergreen branches, corn stalks, or bamboo.

3. During the entire festival, we live in these temporary dwellings as much as possible.

4. It is a *mitzvah* to eat all meals in the *succah* unless it rains, snows, or is uncomfortably hot. Many people do not eat or drink anything outside the *succah*.

5. Before *Shabbos*, we put up an *eruv* (rabbinic boundary) to unite the *succah* and the kitchen where the meals are prepared into a single domain.

---

[46] The difference between the *mitzvah* of *mikvah* and succah is that the *mikvah* serves as a means to an end i.e., purification and/or the resumption of family life, while the *mitzvah* of *succah* is an end to itself.

6. Many people have the custom of decorating the *succah* beautifully. They also prepare fancy dishes and bring out their finest dishes to dress the *succah* table.

7. It is a *mitzvah* to have guests in one's *succah* for each meal.

8. Before you eat an ounce or more of bread, cake or other food made from the five grains, or fruit that the Land of Israel is known for, such as figs, dates, pomegranates, and grapes, you should make the following blessing:

Baruch Atoh Ado-noi Elo-heinu	"Blessed are You, L-rd our G-d,
Melech HaOlam	King of the universe
Asher Kiddeshanu	Who has sanctified us
B'mitzvosav Vitzvivanu	with His commandments,
Leshev b'succah.	commanding us to dwell in the Succah."

The Four Kinds

A most beautiful and meaningful *mitzvah* of *Succos* is the "the taking of the four kinds." The Torah commands us (*Vayikra* 23:40), "You shall take on the first day the fruit of a goodly tree, branches of palms, boughs of myrtles, and willows of the brook, and you shall rejoice before the L-rd your G-d seven days." The four plants are the *esrog* (citron), *lulav* (palm branch), *hadassim* (myrtles) and *aravos* (willows).

Our sages have found deep symbolism in this *mitzvah.* For example, the myrtle's shape corresponds to the eyes, the willow's shape corresponds to the mouth, the *esrog's* shape corresponds to the heart, and the *lulav's* shape corresponds to the spine. Binding

181

them together teaches us that all our organs, limbs and faculties should be dedicated to G-d.

Also, each of the four kinds corresponds to a different type of person. On one hand, literally, the *esrog* has both a refreshing taste (Torah knowledge) and a delightful fragrance (good deeds). It corresponds to the person who excels in both Torah learning and performing good deeds. On the other hand, literally, the willow has neither taste nor smell. It corresponds to the person who studies Torah and performs a minimum of good deeds, but does not excel in either. The fruit of the *lulav* has a taste but no smell. This corresponds to the person who excels in Torah learning, but not good deeds. The myrtle has a smell, but no taste. This corresponds to the person who excels in good deeds but not Torah learning.

Despite their differences, the Torah instructs us to take these four species and bind them, for they complement one another. Similarly, one Jew complements another. In addition, the *mitzvah* teaches us that unity among Jews helps bring blessings from above. Here are some laws associated with this *mitzvah*:

1. This *mitzvah* is performed every day of *Succos* except *Shabbos*.

2. Ideally, it should be done early in the day but is permissible until sunset.

3. To perform the *mitzvah*, take the *lulav*, *haddasim* and *aravos* the right hand and make the following blessing.

Baruch Atoh Ado-noi Elo-heinu	"Blessed are You, L-rd our G-d,
Melech HaOlam	King of the universe
Asher Kiddeshanu	Who has sanctified us
B'mitzvosav Vitzvivanu	with His commandments,
Al natilas lulav.	commanding us to take the *lulav*."

The first time you perform this *mitzvah*, you should also say *Shecheyanu*.

4. After pronouncing the blessing, take the *esrog* in the left hand and hold all the species together with both hands, moving them in six directions. According to *Kabbalah* and *Chassidus*, a person faces east and waves the lulav and esrog to the South, North, East, Up, Down, and West.

5. A left-handed person takes the *lulav* and other species in the left hand and the *esrog* in the right hand.

6. While women are not obligated in this *mitzvah*, they typically perform it throughout *Succos*.

7. When "taking the four kinds" one should be careful to have the hand free of gloves, rings, etc.

Simchas Bais HaSho'eva (Joy at the Place of the Water Drawing)

When the Holy Temple stood, one highlight of *Succos* was the celebration of water-drawing. During the rest of the year, the *Cohainim* (priests) would offer wine as part of the service. They pour wine into a special opening on top of the Altar. On *Succos*, the *Cohainim* also poured water. The water-drawing ceremony actually began on the eve of the second day of *Succot*. The outer court of the Bais HaMikdash was brilliantly lit with torches. *Cohainim* and *Leviim* (Levites) would dance in a procession around the courtyard accompanied by musicians. The celebration lasted all night. The next morning, the procession accompanied a chosen priest to the pool of Siloam in Jerusalem, where he would draw water and return with it to the Holy Temple. The Talmud states, "whoever has not seen the joy at the place of the water-drawing has never seen true joy in his life." (Succah 51)

The water-drawing ceremony was obviously exciting, lively, and colorful. But what made it more joyous? According to *Kabbalah* and *Chassidus*, wine represents intellect and understanding. It has taste, an aroma, and an ability to influence a person. Water, by comparison, symbolizes the pure and simple acceptance of G-d's will. This pure acceptance comes from within, yet it can express itself in joy that breaks all boundaries.

Yom Tov and the Intermediate Days

Outside Israel, *Succos* lasts eight days. The first two and last two days are *yom tov* (holidays). The third through seventh days are called *chol hamoed*, "intermediate days." During this time, we continue eating in the *succah* and saying special prayers. However, we do not light candles or make *kiddush*. In general, only very necessary work may be done.

The last intermediate day is *Hoshana Rabbah*. It is customary to stay awake the night of *Hoshana Rabbah* to learn portions of the Torah, and recite Psalms. In the morning, we open the Holy Ark, take out a Torah, and circle the reading table seven times while holding the *lulav* and *esrog*. Each time that we circle the reading table, we read prayers, *hoshanas* asking G-d for His blessings.

Although the gates of heaven "officially" closed at the end of the Yom Kippur, we ask G-d to open them one last time on *Hoshana Rabbah* and grant us a good year. For this reason, we beat the *hoshanos* (willow branches) several times on the floor after our prayers. This helps to "sweeten" any harsh judgments.

Hoshana Rabbah culminates in the holiday of *Shemini Atzeres*, the "Eighth Day of Assembly."

Shemini Atzeres

Shemini Atzeres corresponds to the eighth day of *Succos*, yet it is a separate *yom tov* in its own right. Rashi, one of our greatest sages, compared *Shemini Atzeres* to a king who held a special feast for his beloved son. For a full week, the king celebrated his love for his son with all his citizens. After this week, the king said to his son: "Your parting is difficult for me. Please stay another day and we will celebrate together, you and I."

The above parable can be linked to the name of the holiday itself. *Atzeres* means "holding back." During the time of the Holy Temple, the Jewish people brought 70 oxen as sacrifices during *Succos*, corresponding to the 70 nations of the world. On the eighth day, only one ox was brought as a sacrifice to emphasize the unique relationship between G-d and His loyal children, the Jews.

Outside of Israel, we eat a final meal in the *succah* on *Shemini Atzeres*. Some go into the *succah* only for *kiddush* in the morning. Either way, we do not say the blessing over the *succah*.

Simchas Torah

In Israel, *Shemini Atzeres* and *Simchas Torah*, the holiday of "Rejoicing with the Torah" are celebrated on the same day. Outside the Land of Israel, *Simchas Torah* occurs the day after *Shemini Atzeres*.

On *Simchas Torah*, all the Torah scrolls are brought out from the ark, and all of the men circle the reading table seven times, taking turns holding the holy Torah scrolls. During *Simchas Torah*, we dance and sing to express our love for the holy Torah.

According to *Kabbalah* and *Chassidus*, the seven *hakafos* "circuits around the reading table" correspond to the seven lower *sefiros* in the chain-like order of the worlds, as well as the seven emotional attributes within man. Dancing these seven *hakafos* on *Simchas Torah* has the ability to draw down "buckets full" of blessings for the entire year.

On *Simchas Torah,* all males over Bar Mitzvah age are called up to the Torah. Even young boys are all called up together for a special *aliya*. During the morning of *Simchas Torah*, the last portion of the Torah scroll is read. Immediately, another person is called up to a second scroll, and we begin the Torah again with *Beraishis bara Elo-him*, "In the beginning,"

The cycle of life as guided by the Torah continues. For in truth, we never finish learning Torah. It is the eternal force that has connected the Jews to G-d for over 3,000 years, and will continue to connect the Jews to G-d through the coming of *Moshiach*.

Cheshvan

There are no holidays; although there is a tradition that G-d promised to appease the month by having the Holy Temple dedicated in Cheshvan.

Kislev-Teves

Chanukah

Chanukah celebrates the victory of the Jews over their Syrian-Greek oppressors in 165 BCE. When the victorious Jews entered the Holy Temple to re-kindle the *menorah*, they found that the enemy had defiled the oil. What many people don't realize is that, under such conditions, the Jews could have lit the menorah with defiled oil, especially since it would take another eight days to obtain olive oil that was pure.

However, the Jews wanted to perform the *mitzvah* in the most beautiful and acceptable manner. Miraculously, they discovered a small jar of olive oil buried in the ruins. It was sealed with the stamp of the High Priest, and although it provided only enough oil to burn for one day, the Jews lit the menorah anyway. Miraculously, the light from this oil lasted eight days.

Why did the Jews have to find oil that was untouched by the Greeks? The answer holds the key to understanding the true victory (and miracle) of *Chanukah*. According to our sages, the Greeks were not trying to kill all the Jews. Nor were they against

Jewish culture or against the Torah as a source of knowledge. They wanted to stamp out our belief in the Torah as G-dly wisdom. Specifically, they wanted to eliminate our observance of commandments, like circumcision and *Shabbos* that were not based on human understanding. With Judaism reduced to a rational philosophy, the Jewish people would easily be assimilated into the Greek culture.

This explains why it was so important to find *pure*, untouched oil. According to *Kabbalah* and *Chassidus*, the small cruise of oil symbolizes the G-dly spark, not only in Judaism, but in every Jew. This G-dly spark can be concealed. It can be buried. But it can never be defiled. Our job is to bring our G-dly spark into the open so that it lights up our homes and our surroundings.

Laws and Customs of Chanukah

A *menorah* should have places for eight flames in a row. The places should be on the same level and should be separate so that we can tell how many wicks are lit. In addition to eight places for candles or oil, the menorah needs a place for the *shamash*, "helping" light. It is placed higher or before the other eight.

On the first night of *Chanukah*, we light one flame on the right side. The next night, we light a second candle or container of oil and a wick. We add these candles from right to left. However, we light the new flame first each night, moving from left (the newest candle) back to the right. The *Chanukah* flames are not lit directly but rather from the flame of the *shamas*. If no *menorah* is available, you can line up small metal caps or small glass cups to hold oil and floating wicks.

Some people place their *menorah* in a window facing a public thoroughfare; others place it in the doorway, opposite the *mezuzah*.

It is best to burn oil to recall the miracles. Candles may be used instead, but not electric lights.

The flames are kindled with the appropriate blessing at either twilight or dark, depending on family custom. In either case, they must burn for a half an hour after nightfall.

On Friday night, *Chanukah* lights must be lit before the *Shabbos* candles. To make sure that they will continue burning after dark, we use larger candles or more oil than usual. On Saturday night, we light the menorah after *havdalah*. The man of the house may light for the household. If he does not light, his wife can.

Children, as well as other adults, can light their own *menorahs*.

It is customary to eat foods fried in oil (donuts, potato pancakes, etc.) during the holiday to recall the miracles associated with the oil. On *Chanukah*, we have a custom to eat dairy. It recalls the brave act of Yehudis, daughter of the High Priest who lived during the Greek rule. At the time, the Greeks would claim any Jewish bride before she married her husband. The Jewish men felt helpless to change the situation. In defiance, Yehudis took matters into her own hands. She met a cruel Greek general under the guise of offering him information. She then fed him wine and dairy foods to make him sleepy, cut off his head, placed it in a basket, and returned to the Jewish lines. Her act spurred the bravery of the men and saved many lives.

It is also a custom to distribute *Chanukah gelt* "money" to family members, especially on the fifth night of *Chanukah*. The fifth night of *Chanukah* never falls on *Shabbos*, so it is a custom to add extra holiness to it by giving *tzedakah*. The *Chanukah gelt* is also intended to reward children for learning.

In addition, it is a custom to play with the *dreidel* to recall the Jewish children who learned Torah in spite of the Greeks. Whenever a Greek soldier would approach them, the children would take out their tops and appear to be playing games. The four letters on the *dreidel*, *nun gimmel, hei*, and *shin*, stand for the words *Nes Gadol Haya Sham*, "a great miracle happened there." The numerical value of those letters is the same as "*Moshiach*," the True Messiah. This teaches us that self-sacrifice for Judaism will help bring *Moshiach*.

10th *of Teves*

On this day in the year 586 before the Common Era, the Babylonian king, Nebuchadnezzar besieged Jerusalem. This led to the destruction of the First Temple and the exile of the Jewish people. On this day, we fast from dawn to sunset. We also recite special prayers.

Shvat

Tu B'Shvat

The fifteenth day of the Hebrew month *Shvat* is New Year's day
(*Rosh Hashana*) for trees. The day marks the beginning of the
spring season in the Land of Israel. At this time, G-d judges each
tree and declares its future. This holiday also holds an important
lesson for man.

In *Devorim* 20:19, the Torah associates man to tree of the field.
Through the comparison, the Torah teaches us that, like a tree,
man too must produce fruit. The fruits of man are Torah and
good deeds. Just as fruit fulfills the purpose of the tree, so do
Torah and *mitzvos* fulfill the purpose of man in this world.

On *Tu B'Shvat*, it is customary to eat fruits of the Land of Israel:
olives, dates, grapes, figs, and pomegranates. We also eat a new
fruit of the season for the first time so that we can say the blessing
shehechiyanu.

Adar

Our sages say that, "When *Adar* enters, we increase in joy." *Adar*
contains the holiday of Purim. During leap years, we add a 13th
month, *Adar II*. The reason is that the Jewish calendar is based
on both the lunar and solar cycles. The lunar cycle is used to set
time. Each year consists of 12 months and lasts 354 days. The
solar year is used to track the seasons: spring, summer, winter,

and fall[47]. To reconcile the 11 days that separate lunar and solar calendars, we add a month, *Adar II*, seven times in 19 years.

Purim

Purim commemorates the miracle that happened in Persia in the years between the First and Second Temples. Mordechai the Jew refuses to bow before King Achashveiros' advisor Haman. Outraged, Haman plots to kill Mordechai along with the entire Jewish nation. Haman cunningly tells the king that the Jewish people have no use or value. In response, the king puts the fate of the Jewish people into his hands. Haman sends messengers throughout 127 provinces commanding them to kill the Jews on the 13th of the Jewish month of *Adar*. Haman selected *Adar* by casting lots (*pur* in Persian.[48])

However, unknown to Haman, the King's new wife, Esther, is Jewish. Mordechai tell her of Haman's plans and she devises a plan of her own. She tells the Jewish people to fast. She and her maids will also fast and ask for Hashem's salvation. Then she invites Haman and the King to a meal. There she reveals her Jewish identify and pleads for her life and the lives of her people. Enraged that his queen was being threatened, the King orders Haman hung and empowers the Jews to defend themselves against their enemies.

---

[47] If we continuously followed the lunar cycle, we would "lose" 11 days a year. Eventually, we would end up celebrating Passover in the fall or early winter, not spring. To avoid this, we add a second month of Adar. This moves Passover "back" to the spring where it belongs.
[48] Haman was overjoyed when the lot fell in Adar because that month is associated with the death of Moses. However, Haman did not realize that Moses was also born on the same date 120 years earlier. So far from being a negative day, it was an auspicious time Above.

The *mitzvos* associated with Purim actually start on the *Shabbos* before the holiday. At that time, we read *Parshas Zochor*. This Torah portion describes how Amalek attacked the Jewish people after the Exodus from Egypt. It also commands us to blot out the name of Amalek. Haman was a descendant of Amalek.

The day before *Purim*, we fast the entire day, from 72 minutes before sunrise to nightfall. This recalls the fast that Esther and the Jewish people undertook on the 13th of Adar, the day that the Jews battled and destroyed Haman's evil forces.

On *Purim* evening and morning, we read the story of *Purim* from a parchment scroll called the *Megillas[49] ("scroll of") Esther*. All men and women, including boys over age thirteen and girls over age twelve, should hear the *Megillah*. Younger boys and girls should be trained to hear the *Megillah,* as well. Since Haman descended from Amalek and the Torah commands us to blot out the memory of Amalek, we customarily make noise whenever the reader mentions Haman's name along with a description (*Haman HaRasha* "Haman the wicked" or *Haman HaAgagi* "Haman the Agaggite").

Interestingly, the *Megillah* does not contain one of the holy names of G-d.[50] Yet it is clear that Divine Providence shaped the events of *Purim* from beginning to end. This teaches us that G-d's Providence continues to direct events, even though it may be concealed within the "natural" order of the world.)

---

[49] There are five *Megilla* scrolls: *Ruth, Esther, Eicha* (Lamentations), *Shir HaShirim* (Song of Songs) and *Koheles* (Ecclesiastes)

[50] However, the sages state that whenever the Megillah mentions HaMelech, "the King," it is referring to G-d.

During the day of Purim, we send *mishloach manos*, "food packages." Everyone should send at least two types of prepared food or fruit to (at least) one friend. (Women send *mishloach manos* to women; men to men.).

During *Purim*, we also give *matanos l'evyonim*, "gifts to the poor." You should give coins to at least two poor people or two worthy organizations.

At some point during *Purim*, we hold a festive meal to celebrate the victory over our enemies. The Talmud states that one should drink until he is "no longer able to tell the difference between 'blessed be Mordechai' and 'cursed be Haman. This refers to a level that is higher than intellect. At this level, divinity exists as the true reality. It also refers to the amount of wine that can make a person drowsy.

It is a custom to eat *hamantashen*, three-cornered pastries on the day. Some say that *hamantashen* were filled with poppy seeds to recall how Queen Esther ate seeds to keep kosher in the palace. The pastry, with its filling hidden inside, symbolizes the hidden miracles of Purim.

According to *Kabbalah* and *Chassidus*, all the heavenly blessings that a Jew can draw down on Yom Kippur through prayer and *teshuva* can be brought down through joy on Purim. This can be read into the word, *Yom Kippurim,* which can also be read as "a day like Purim."

Purim serves to remind us that only 30 days remain until *Pesach*.

The holidays of *Purim* and *Chanukah* were "set" by the Rabbis. *Chanukah* recalls the time when our enemies tried to destroy our connection to the Torah as G-dly Wisdom. Therefore, we celebrate *Chanukah* by reciting Psalms of praise and by lighting a *Chanukah* lamp to symbolize the light of G-dly Wisdom. We also spin the *dreidel* from above. This indicates that miracles came from G-d as He is above nature.

Purim, by contrast, recalls the time when our enemies tried to destroy our bodies. Therefore, we celebrate *Purim* by eating, drinking and whirling the *grogger* (noisemaker). This indicates that miracles came from G-d within nature.

Nissan

Pesach

Pesach celebrates the birth of the Jewish nation with the Exodus from Egypt. The Torah calls Pesach *z'man cheiruseinu*, the "season of our freedom." *Chassidus* explains that the Hebrew word for Egypt is *Mitzrayim*. It is related to the word *metzarim* meaning "limitations." On Pesach, G-d granted the Jewish nation the ability to rise above and beyond the limitations of the natural world. This is true historically. For example, Mark Twain wrote:

> If the statistics are right, the Jews constitute but *one percent* of the human race. It suggests a nebulous dim puff of stardust lost in the blaze of the Milky Way. Properly the Jew ought hardly to be heard of; but he is heard of, has always been heard of. He is as prominent on the planet as any other people, and his commercial importance is extravagantly out

of proportion to the smallness of his bulk. His contributions to the world's list of great names in literature, science, art, music, finance, medicine, and abstruse learning are also away out of proportion to the weakness of his numbers. He has made a marvelous fight in this world, in all the ages; and has done it with his hands tied behind him. He could be vain of himself, and be excused for it. The Egyptian, the Babylonian, and the Persian rose, filled the planet with sound and splendor, then faded to dream-stuff and passed away; the Greek and the Roman followed, and made a vast noise, and they are gone; other peoples have sprung up and held their torch high for a time, but it burned out, and they sit in twilight now, or have vanished. The Jew saw them all, beat them all, and is now what he always was, exhibiting no decadence, no infirmities of age, no weakening of his parts, no slowing of his energies, no dulling of his alert and aggressive mind. All things are mortal but the Jew; all other forces pass, but he remains. What is the secret of his immortality[51]?

On *Pesach*, G-d also granted the Jewish nation the ability to rise above and beyond the spiritual limitations. In fact, the word Pesach means "to skip over." It typically recalls the time when G-d "skipped over" the houses of the Jews in Egypt and killed the first-born among the Egyptians. But Pesach also hints to the Jews ability to make spiritual leaps in one's conduct and service.

---

[51] Twain, Mark, The Man That Corrupted Hadleyburg and Other Stories and Essays (New York: Harper & Brothers, 1900).

According to *Kabbalah*, *Pesach* is composed of two Hebrew words that mean, "the mouth speaks." On one level, the slavery of the Jewish people prevented them from being able to praise G-d. On *Pesach*, the Jewish people, and their ability to speak, were liberated. On a deeper level, the mouth speaks refers to the *sefirah* of *malchus*, kingship. A king rules through his decrees. When the Jewish people were in exile, the Egyptians prevented them from worshipping G-d. As a result, G-d's *sefirah* of *malchus* was also in exile. Once the Jewish people became a free nation, they were able to follow the decrees of the King of Kings without interference. In a sense, the *sefirah* of *malchus* was redeemed with them.

Preparing for the Holiday

In general, many people start preparing for a holiday at least 30 days before it occurs. At that time, they begin reviewing the laws of the upcoming festival. While this is true of all holidays, it is especially important for Pesach because of all its laws.

For example, we are forbidden to possess any type of leaven (called *chometz*) or leavened product on Pesach. This includes bread, crackers, cereal, alcoholic beverages, and dozens of other food products. Even the tiniest amount is prohibited[52]. Therefore, we begin "cleaning for *Pesach*" many weeks before the holiday. To avoid any problems, it is the custom to have a separate set of dishes for *Pesach*. We put *chometz* in out-of-the-way places so that we "forget" that we transferred ownership during the holiday. We clean clothes, suitcases, books, cars, or any other

---

[52] When we refer to *chometz*, we speak about dough that has the ability to rise. Spiritually, it refers to one's ego. Before Pesach, we must get rid of our self-centered desires, because this is the only way to unite with the Jewish people, and ultimately, to G-d.

place that might contain *chometz*. We also contract with a competent Rabbinic authority to sell any *chometz* we possess to a non-Jew.

By the day before *Pesach*, one's dwelling should be free of *chometz*. To make sure, we search for *chometz* at night. Some communities have a custom to "hide" ten pieces of bread or other *chometz* so that the person searching for the *chometz* will actually find something. (The 10 pieces of bread symbolize the 10 *sefiros* from the side of unholiness.) On the morning of Pesach, we remove these pieces and any other *chometz* from the house and burn it.

From approximately 9:30 A.M. the day before *Pesach*[53], we avoid eating *chometz*. About an hour later, we should stop benefiting from *chometz* in any manner and not possess any *chometz* at all. (If *these* deadlines are missed, consult your rabbi immediately.)

During the day of Pesach, we avoid eating *matzoh*, as well any of the other foods on the *seder* plate, such as eggs, apples and nuts, onions (or potatoes), etc.

All first-born males should fast on the day of Pesach to recall the tenth plague in Egypt. It killed all the Egyptian firstborn, while sparing the first-born of the Jews. Many communities have a custom to finish a tractate of the Talmud and have some food after. Since participating in this event is a *mitzvah*, we may associate with it because a first-born, who de facto broke the fast, is no longer obligated to fast.

---

[53] Check the Hebrew calendar for exact time in your location.

Pesach evening begins with the holiday prayers. Some communities follow the evening services by reciting psalms of praise, known as *Hallel*. After services, everyone hurries home to enjoy the special Passover meal called the *Seder*. (All the foods necessary for the *Seder* should be prepared before *Yom Tov* to avoid *halachic* questions.)

The Seder

The Hebrew word *Seder* means "order" and refers to the 15 parts of the meal:

Kadish – Kiddush over wine

Urchatz – Washing hands before eating *Karpas*

Karpas – Eating vegetable onions (or potatoes)

Yachatz – Dividing the middle *matzah*, saving part for later

Maggid – Reciting the *Haggadah*

Rochtza – Washing the hands before the meal

Motzi – Blessing over *matzah*

Matzah – Special blessing over *mitzvah* of eating *matzah*

Maror – Special blessing over *mitzvah* of eating bitter herbs

Korech – Eating matzah and maror together

Shulchan Oruch - Eating the yom tov meal

Tzafun – Eating the *afikoman*, part that was saved for later

Barech – Grace after meals

Hallel – Saying psalms of praise

Nirtza – Prayer that our *Seder* was acceptable before G-d

Every part of the *Seder* has deep meaning and symbolism. To helps us understand and experience the seder, we read a special book called the *Hagadah*. It recounts the events and miracles associated with the liberation from Egypt. (The word *Hagadah* means "telling.")

According to Rabbi Tzvi Elimelech of Dinov, Moses originally wrote the *Hagadah* to teach his children the story of Pesach. Over the centuries, the sages added sections to emphasize certain points. The *Hagadah* ends with the words "Next year in Jerusalem," meaning that by this time next year, we should be celebrating the *Seder* in Jerusalem.

Here are some of the lessons associated with the Seder:

During the Seder, we use three *matzos*. They correspond to our Patriarchs Abraham, Isaac and Jacob. Many communities only use special *shmurah* "guarded" *matzah* on Pesach. To avoid the possibility of *chametz*, special precautions are taken to guard the wheat from touching water from the time of reaping.

In addition to the *matzah*, we drink four special cups of wine during the *Seder*. Wine symbolizes freedom and happiness. The four cups of wine correspond to the four expressions found in the Torah: *And I brought out- And I delivered- And I redeemed- And I took*. Yet there is a fifth expression of redemption used in the Torah: *And I brought*. This refers to the ultimate redemption.

Since our sages say that the Prophet Elijah may be given the honor of announcing Messiah, we call the fifth cup of wine, the Cup of Elijah in his honor. (We don't drink the wine from this cup. After the Seder, we pour it back into the bottle.)

The *Seder* plate holds many other symbolic foods. The chicken neck recalls the Pesach sacrifice that was offered in the Holy Temple. The egg recalls the holiday sacrifice offered in the Holy Temple. Horseradish (*maror*) represents the bitterness of slavery. The mixture of apples, nuts, and wine called *charoses* represents the mortar that the Jewish people used to make bricks for the Egyptians. The *chazeres* combines romaine lettuce and horseradish and also recalls the bitterness of exile. It is used to fulfill the *mitzvah* of eating *matzah* and *moror* together. *Karpas* is a vegetable that is dipped in salt water to arouse the curiosity of children and guests at the *Seder* table. On one hand, dipping into a condiment is a sign of wealth. On the other hand, we dip the vegetable into salt water which represent the tears we shed in slavery and exile.

At the end of the meal, we eat *the afikoman* "set aside" *matzah*. The *afikoman* (at least 2 ounces per adult), reminds us of the Pesach Sacrifice that we ate during the times of the Holy Temple.

By the way, when the Jews left Egypt, they couldn't wait for their dough to rise. The flat, tasteless *matzah* was called *lechem oni*, "bread of a poor person." On a deeper level, *matzah* symbolizes selflessness. According to the *Zohar, matzah* is known as "the food of faith" and the "food for healing" because it connects us to Hashem, who is the source of all blessings, including heath.

Nissan-Iyar

Sefiros HaOmer

On the second day of Passover, the Torah commands us to offer a measure (omer) of barley as a meal offering in the Temple. We are then commanded to count 49 days and celebrate the holiday of *Shavuos*. This time period is called *Sefiros HaOmer*, the counting of the days of the *Omer*. We use this time to prepare ourselves to receive the Torah. Each day, we elevate ourselves one step higher than the day before.

Pesach Sheni

Thirty days after celebrating *Pesach*, we have another opportunity called *Pesach Sheni*, "second *Pesach*." When the Jews left Egypt, some Jews were spiritually impure. As a result, they could not participate in the Pesach offering. They came to Moses to ask how they too could be included in the *mitzvah*. G-d was pleased with their request and gave them another opportunity to bring a *Pesach* sacrifice. *Pesach Sheni* teaches us that it is never too late. We must never lose hope; G-d always gives us another chance.

Though *Pesach Sheni* is not a *yom tov*, it is still a special day. It is customary to eat *matzah*. However, there is no prohibition against bread or any other food.

These days have another meaning. During the *Omer* period, many of Rabbi Akiva's students died. Our Sages then declared that these days should be commemorated as partial mourning days. Rejoicing is curtailed. It is customary not to make weddings, listen to live music, or take a haircut during this time.

Lag B'Omer

The Hebrew letters *"lamed gimmel"* are numerically equivalent to 33. On the 33rd day of the Omer, the epidemic stopped. This is a day of great rejoicing. Weddings and other celebrations are permitted. Also, boys who have reached the age of three during the 32 days of the Omer now receive their ceremonial hair cut, the *upsherenish*, on this day.

The 33rd day of the *Omer* is also the *hilula* (day of praise - *Yahrzeit*) of our holy sage, Rabbi Shimon Bar Yochai. The *hilula-Yahrzeit* of a great person is often marked with celebration, since every year, the person's soul ascends to greater heights in the eternal world. Rabbi Shimon Bar Yochai is the author of the *Zohar*, one of the earliest and most important written sources of *Kabbalah* and Jewish mysticism. It is written about Rabbi Shimon Bar Yochai that during his lifetime, no rainbow appeared. The rainbow symbolizes G-d's promise not to destroy the world with a flood. While Rabbi Shimon Bar Yochai was alive, his merit protected the world so it did not need the reminder and the guarantee of the rainbow. To remember the greatness of Rabbi Shimon Bar Yochai, it has become a custom that on Lag B'Omer, children are often taken on outings in the parks or woods.

Sivan

Shavuos

Shavuos means "weeks" and refers to the harvest of the first wheat crop. On *Shavuos*, the priests would bring two loaves of wheat as an offering.

Shavuos also marks the Giving of the Torah on Mt. Sinai. Until Sinai, the Jewish nation followed the traditions of Abraham, Isaac, and Jacob. The Jewish nation also received certain laws from G-d, such as the laws of *Shabbos* and civil laws, when they encamped by the waters of Mara. On *Shavuos*, all these traditions and laws were reintroduced with the Giving of the Torah.

Shavuos marks an essential change in the Jewish people and the world. Before *kabbalas HaTorah*, "receiving the Torah," the upper worlds and the earthly world remained apart. The Jewish people could not change the nature of an object. When the Torah was given, G-d "inclined" the heavens and "elevated" the world. At that point, the barrier disappeared. The Torah enabled us to change the nature of a physical object by "charging" it with spirituality and holiness.

For example, a scribe can take leather, parchment, and ink and by following the laws of the Torah turn them into *tefillin*. The very same leather, ink, and parchment have attained a degree of holiness that was not there before. Now they have become holy objects and must be treated in a special way. Similarly, we can take a building and consecrate it as a synagogue. At that point, its status has been changed. It is has been permeated with G-dliness.

Interestingly, the Torah does not link the giving of the Torah to *Shavuos*. It also doesn't set a date for the holiday. Instead, the Torah states that, "You shall count seven weeks, from the day when the sickle is first put to the standing grain. You shall then keep the feast of Weeks in honor of the L-rd your G-d....."

However, we know that the giving of the Torah occurred on the sixth of Sivan, corresponding to that date.

The question is: why didn't the Torah specify when it was given? There are several answers. If the Torah specified a date, we might limit Torah study to that time of year or that specific holiday. By not mentioning the date, the Torah is hinting that the "giving the Torah" can, and does, occur every day. It is a "present" in both senses of the word.

By Divine Providence, *Shavuos* is also the anniversary of the passing of King David, who is the forefather of *Moshiach*. It is also the day when the Baal Shem Tov, the founder of the Chassidic movement, passed away.

In addition to "weeks," the word *Shavuos* can be also be translated as "oaths." According to the *Midrash*, G-d offered the Torah to the nations of the world. Each nation wanted to know what the Torah contained. When G-d told them, each nation refused G-d's gift. When G-d offered the Torah to the Jews, they immediately replied, *Naaseh vNishma*, "we will obey and then we will understand through our intellect."

Another *Midrash* relates that, right before the giving of the Torah, G-d asked the Jewish people, "Who will guarantee the Torah? How can I be assured that the Torah would be cherished and observed throughout the generations?"

The Jewish people offered many possible guarantors, from the patriarchs to the prophets, but G-d was not satisfied. When the Jewish people suggested, "Our children," G-d agreed. *Shavuos* commemorates our commitment to do and then understand, and our willingness to give our children as guarantors. The Hebrew word "*Shavuos*" refers to these oaths. The word is also related to the word *sova*, which means "full" or "satiated." According to *Kabbalah* and *Chassidus*, taking an oath empowers the person to fulfill it. As Jews, we have the ability to observe the Torah and to educate our children in its ways.

Rabbi Levi Yitzchok of Berditchev taught that the three holidays of *Pesach*, *Shavuos*, and *Sukkos* give us the opportunity to rectify problems in three areas. If a person spent money inappropriately, one can "rectify" this by spending money for *Pesach*. If a person ate food in an inappropriate manner, one can rectify this by eating kosher food with the proper intentions in the *Succah*. If a person didn't act appropriately with one's wife, *Shavuos* gives him the opportunity to rectify this; for *Shavuos* represents the "marriage" of the Jewish people and G-d.

Shavuos Customs

On *Shavuos* night, it is customary for men and boys over 13 to study Torah all night long to show our eagerness to receive the Torah. The Torah reading on *Shavuos* describes the giving of the 10 Commandments at Mount Sinai. When the reader comes to the 10 Commandments, all congregants stand.

On the first day of *yom tov*, it is customary to eat a dairy meal. (Many people wait an hour after eating dairy and have a meat meal.) If the meat meal is eaten first, one must wait six hours before eating dairy.) Soft cheese dishes, particularly blintzes, are traditionally served. When the Jews received the Torah, they received the laws of *kashrus* since they did not have kosher utensils or kosher meat, they ate dairy.

Shavuos is also the festival of first fruits. The first fruits were brought to the Holy Temple in beautifully arranged baskets, and offered with great pageantry and an inspiring ceremony. For this reason, some people also have the custom on *Shavuos* of eating a "new" fruit and saying the blessing *shehechiyanu*.

On *Shavuos*, many people also read the story of Ruth. She was a convert who exemplified a sincere commitment to our faith. She is also the ancestor of King David.

Tammuz

Shiva Asar b' Tammuz

Five tragedies occurred throughout history on the 17th of Tammuz.

1. Moses broke the first tablets of the Ten Commandments.

2. The priests stopped offering the daily burnt sacrifice in the Temple.

3. Nebuchadnezzar's troops breached the walls of Jerusalem.

4. The Roman general Apostomus burned a Torah.

5. The Romans placed an idol in the Temple.

It is the custom to fast from dawn to nightfall on this day and to recite special prayers. This day also begins three weeks of semi-mourning over the destruction of the Temple. During this time, we don't hold weddings or engage in other joyous occasions. The three-week period ends with the 10th of Av.

Av

Tisha B'Av

This day recalls the destruction of both the First and Second Holy Temples. On this day, we are forbidden to eat, drink, wash, wear leather shoes, or have marital relations. The fast starts before sunset on the eighth and runs until nightfall on the ninth of Av. It is the custom to read *Eicha*, Lamentations, and *kinos*, "elegies." Men postpone wearing a *tallis,* "prayer shawl," and *tefillin* until the afternoon of the ninth.

Tisha B'Av represents the saddest day of the Jewish year. According to our sages, the Second Holy Temple was destroyed because of *sinas chinam*, unwarranted hatred between Jews. By showing unwarranted affection and love of one's fellow, we can rectify this.

As bleak as *Tisha B'Av* is, the day also contains a ray of hope. According to Jewish law, the only way one can destroy a synagogue is for the purpose of building another in its place. So too, the destruction of the first Holy Temple enabled the Second to be built. Similarly, the destruction of the Second will lead to the building of the Third Holy Temple. May it occur speedily.

15th of Av

This holiday is among the happiest in the calendar. On this day, the Jewish people who were condemned to die in the desert stopped dying. It was a custom for Jewish girls to go out into the fields and dance before Jewish boys to encourage them to marry. Interestingly, the girls exchanged clothes so that a boy could not tell who was rich or who was poor.

For Further Reading:

The Book of Our Heritage
Eliyahu KiTov
Feldheim Publishing Co., 1979

Rite and Reason
Rabbi Shmel Gelbard
Feldheim Publishers, 2000

Guidelines (Series)
R. Elozor Barclay
Feldheim Publishers, 2000

17. The Jewish Lifecycle

In Pirke Avos (6:5), we read "Do not yearn for the table of kings, for your table is greater than theirs, and your crown is greater than theirs....." All the external wealth, glory, and strength of kings cannot compare to the inner wealth, the inner glory, and the inner strength of the Jewish people and the Jewish way of life. One doesn't have to look any further than the royal family of England. Millions watched the fairytale marriage of the Crown Prince of England and his blushing bride, as they were united with all the pomp and circumstance that the Court of S. James could provide. Sadly, pomp and circumstance was all that it could provide, as the world eventually learned.

Similarly, American society worships youth, wealth, and fame. But youth, wealth, and fame are transitory. And the rock star still has to look in the mirror every morning, knowing that he is powerless to stop time or to recapture his past.

Judaism by contrast, is like a diamond with many facets. Each facet represents a milestone in life, and each glows with its own special beauty. It's a beauty that expresses itself in two ways.

There is the pride of the moment, as family, friends, and communities celebrate *simchos*, "joyous occasions" with each other, and support each other during times of stress. Yet there is another dimension. It is the knowledge that the path and the milestones that you are following, have been followed by others before you, and will continue to be followed by others after. Your destiny is part of theirs. No other religion, culture, or community offers such a golden chain of tradition, history, and wisdom. No other set of values balances spirituality with the material aspects of life. No other philosophy honors each stage in man's development, while respecting the others, as well.

Birth

The birth of a child is a time of joy; not just for the parents, but for the entire Jewish nation. Each child possesses a *neshoma* (soul) that can play a part in elevating the world and making it a proper dwelling place for G-d. For this reason, many women add a *Shabbos* candle for every new child in the family because each one represents a new source of light.

According to our sages, Heaven gives parents a special gift of prophecy to name a child. The name reflects the inner powers and personality of the child. At the same time, the name serves as a channel to reveal those powers. Ideally, boys should be named for males and girls should be named for females.

Some people have the custom to add a letter or a second name later on in life to help a person obtain good health or long life. Changing the name can help change the *mazal* (flow of blessings.) The Torah records several instances of names being changed.

Abraham's original name was Avram. G-d changed his name when He blessed him with children. Sara's original name was Sarai. Jacob (Yaakov) became Israel (Yisroel.) And Yoshua became Yehoshua (Joshua.)

Bris

On the eighth day after birth, Jewish boys undergo circumcision. The *bris* represents a covenant, an inviolable contract, between G-d and the Jewish people. The Torah (Genesis 17: 9-12) states, "G-d said to Abraham: You shall keep my covenant, you and your descendants after you throughout their generations...Every male among you shall be circumcised...and it shall be a sign of the covenant between Me and you. He that is eight days old among you shall be circumcised." Abraham was the first person to have a circumcision. In fact, he circumcised himself when he was 99 years old. He also circumcised his son, Yishmael, at 13. Even today, Arabs circumcise their sons at 13. Abraham's son Isaac was first to have a *bris* at eight days.

According to *Chassidus*, nature follows a pattern of sevens. There are seven days in the week. There are seven notes in the musical scale. There are also seven emotional attributes that make up a person. The number eight is higher than nature. For that reason, the *bris* represents a relationship that is above any understanding, e.g., higher than intellect and emotion. Intellect is based on information and influenced by emotions. Today, intellect can help a person to choose one direction. Tomorrow, it can turn a person in a completely different direction. By commanding us to circumcise our children at eight days, G-d is telling us that our relationship does not depend on what we think, but who we are. (Women do not need to have this sign of the covenant because, as we have mentioned before, it is intrinsic. They have a direct and inner connection to a level that is higher than intellect. It is the level of G-d's *ratzon*, "Will.")

The commandment of circumcision is so important that it can be performed on *Shabbos* and even *Yom Kippur*. Only a qualified (i.e., Orthodox) *mohel* should perform a circumcision. There are several reasons for this. Non-Orthodox *mohelim* use a clamp like a cigar-cutter. Not only is it painful, it is also not kosher according to Jewish law. Orthodox *mohelim* use an extremely sharp knife and a shield. The entire process goes quicker, heals faster, and causes less pain.

There's another reason to avoid non-Orthodox *mohelim*. If the whole point is to bring the child into the covenant of Abraham, the *mohel* who represents the parents should observe the *mitzvos* associated with that covenant. Non-Orthodox *mohelim* and non-observant doctors do not qualify.

If a Jewish boy or man was circumcised by a non-Orthodox *mohel*, a Rav should be consulted. If a doctor was used, the person should undergo a procedure called *hatafas dam*, "a drop of blood." The *mohel* draws a tiny drop of blood to rectify the circumcision from a spiritual perspective.

Continuing on a spiritual level, circumcision removes the tendency toward coarseness and opens a person up to holiness. This is the significance of Abraham having a *bris* at 99. The number 100 represents all 10 soul powers in their ultimate state of perfection. Since Abraham hadn't reached that level, he still needed to circumcise himself, to remove the thin layer of skin (attraction to physicality) that remained. Interestingly, the name Abraham has the numerical value of 248. It corresponds to the 248 "limbs" of the body. By comparison, his previous name, Avram, had the value of 243. At that level, Abraham was missing control over five organs, the two eyes, the two ears, and the organ of the *bris*. When Abraham circumcised himself, he gained mastery over his physical being. What's more, he endowed all his descendants with this potential.

Pidyon Ha-Ben

When G-d killed the firstborn sons of Egypt, he saved the firstborn sons of the Jewish people. At that time, G-d sanctified and chose them to serve G-d in the sanctuary. However, after the first-born participated in the episode of the Golden Calf, G-d chose the tribe of Levi to take the place of the firstborn. G-d then ordered Jewish parents to "redeem" each firstborn Israelite by giving a *Cohain* five silver shekels, as the Torah states (*Shemos* 13:13) "and all the firstborn of your sons you should redeem."

Today, we perform this *mitzvah* on the 31st day after the birth of the firstborn. A rabbi asks the father if he wishes to give the child to the *Cohain* or redeem him for five shekels. The father says that he wishes to redeem the child and gives the *Cohain* five silver coins. The *Cohain* usually gives the money to charity.

Upsherenish

Many communities refrain from cutting a boy's hair until the age of three. The Torah compares man to a tree. And just as we refrain from eating fruit from a tree for the first three years, so too, we let the child grow without demanding too much. However, when the child turns three, we cut his hair, leaving the *payos* (sidelocks), and train the child to wear *Tzitsis* and a *yarmulke*.

Bar/Bas Mitzvah

Bar is Aramaic for the Hebrew word *ben*, meaning "son." One who is a bar or bas mitzvah means one who is the "son" or "daughter" of a *mitzvah*; i.e. one who has the duty to fulfill a *mitzvah*. At the age of 13 for a boy or 12 for a girl, one becomes "an adult" and can fulfill communal obligations. For example, a boy dons *tefillin* and is counted as a member of a *minyan*. Similarly, a girl who knows Hebrew can make a *brocha* on behalf of a woman who does not know how to read. It is customary for boys to be called to the Torah on or soon after their 13th birthday. In many communities, boys receive the *maftir* (last) *aliya* on Shabbos, and then recite the *haftorah*, a portion of the prophets.

According to *Kabbalah* and *Chassidus*, the bar or bas mitzvah represents a time of transition. Until this time, a child is primarily influenced by his or her *yetzer hara*, selfish inclination. After bar or bas mitzvah, the *yetzer tov*, one's selfless inclination becomes stronger. Both the numbers 12 and 13 have spiritual significance. Twelve corresponds to the number of tribes, months, and spiritual constellations. It is symbolic of growth and integration, which is the feminine role in Judaism. The number "thirteen" corresponds to G-d's 13 attributes of mercy. It represents potential that must be actualized.

Marriage

The first commandment that G-d gave to man was "be fruitful and multiply." According to *Kabbalah* and *Chassidus*, marriage represents the ultimate state of sanctification, in which husband and wife merge to reach a higher level than each could achieve on his/her own. Out of this level flows a new revelation. On a spiritual level, this new revelation is the establishment of an everlasting home. On a physical level, it refers to the birth of a child. Both aspects of revelation reflect the Divine concept of creating *yesh m'ayin*, something out of nothing.

In Judaism, marriage exists for another purpose: to continue the job of making the world a dwelling place for G-dliness by infusing every act, from the most mundane to the most sublime with holiness. Within this context of marriage, one's emotional, physical, and spiritual needs are still important, but they are not central. Ideally, personal growth and fulfillment come, not at the expense of your partner, but through your partner. Together, both parties become closer to G-d. Needless to say, this is a challenge, especially when society promotes selfish pleasure as the ultimate goal of marriage and life. However, a Jewish marriage tries to keep the feelings of self and others in a healthy balance.

Interestingly, every step in the Jewish marriage ceremony reflects this process of uniting with each other and with G-d.[54] The

---

[54] In fact, the relationship between G-d and the Jewish people is viewed as a marriage; one that took place on Mount Sinai with the Giving of the Torah.

marriage canopy corresponds to the infinite and transcendent aspect of G-dliness, *Or Makif*. The seven blessings correspond to the seven days of creation, the days of the week, the seven times that tefillin straps go around one's arm, and the seven emotional attributes, as the partners seek to draw down this sublime level of holiness into their daily lives. The marriage contract, *ketuba*, serves to formalize this relationship. During the seven days following the marriage ceremony, the bridge and groom are escorted everywhere and treated like the king and queen they are. Each night, it is the custom to enjoy a meal and recite the seven blessings over a cup of wine when a *minyan* (quorum) is present.

The unity between husband and wife continues throughout their lives. In the ideal Jewish marriage, there is no "me." There is only "we," partners working to benefit themselves and the world around them through their spiritual growth. A story told about Rabbi Aryeh Levin[55] illustrates this. Rabbi Levin once took his beloved *Rebbetzin* to the doctor. When the doctor asked the *Rebbetzin* to explain the problem, Rabbi Levin answered for his wife, saying, "Our feet hurt." To Rabbi Levin, his wife's discomfort was his own.

This is one of many differences between the Jewish view of love and the non-Jewish view of love. In the Jewish world, people meet, get married, and begin the process of falling in love, i.e. growing together spiritually and physically. In the non-Jewish world, people meet, fall in love, and (maybe) marry. Their

---

[55] Raz, Simcha; A Tzaddik in Our Time: The Life of Rabbi Aryeh Levin; Feldheim Pub., 2008, p. 50.

relationship exists to satisfy the physical and emotional needs of the participants. The marriage continues as long as both parties' needs are met. When they are not met, the marriage dissolves.

If, G-d forbid, a Jewish marriage does not succeed, the couple must obtain a "*get*," a Jewish bill of divorce. This document dissolves a Jewish marriage. A civil divorce does not. Even if the couple did not get married in a Jewish ceremony, they still need to have a get. For further information, consult your local Orthodox Rabbi.

Family Purity

One of the unique aspects of a Jewish marriage is *taharas hamishpacha*, the laws of family purity. Every month, the moon waxes and wanes. The physical and spiritual natures of both men and women reflect this phenomenon of advance and retreat, closeness and separation. At some point, couples need time to recharge their spiritual, and often physical, energies. *Taharas hamishpacha* provides such an infrastructure for personal rebirth and restoration.

According to the laws of family purity, a woman who has begun to menstruate is forbidden to physically associate with her husband. This "off limits" status continues seven days after the flow stops. The night after the end of seven days, the woman immerses in a *mikvah*, a 200-gallon pool of natural water. At that point, she and her husband resume their marital relationship.

Interestingly, men (who are encouraged, but not obligated) and women visit the *mikvah*. According to *Kabbalah* and *Chassidus*, men should immerse in a *mikvah* daily before worshipping G-d. Even those who don't go daily try to visit the *mikvah* before the high holidays.

The inner concept of *mikvah* is revealed in the Hebrew word *tevilah*, "immersion." When we immerse in a *mikvah*, we nullify our ego before the Creator. We leave the *mikvah* on a higher spiritual level. For this reason, both male (even if circumcised) and female converts immerse in a *mikvah*. On Yom Kippur, the high priest immerses in a *mikvah* five times during the day. Each time, represents another spiritual ascent. *Kabbalah* states that, before ascending to the higher level of the Garden of Eden, one must immerse in *nahar dinur*, a river of fire, to nullify one's connection to the previous level.

In Judaism, the woman is primarily responsible for bringing children, the future of the Jewish people, into the world. As a result, G-d gave her the ability and the *mitzvah* to protect and enhance their spiritual well-being through the *mikvah*. Even if the woman cannot have children, G-d forbid, the waters of the *mikvah* elevate her status in holiness. Separating and uniting monthly also prevents husband and wife from taking each other for granted. Instead, their marriage remains vibrant and alive.

Conversion

Traditional religious law defines a "Jew" as someone who is born of a Jewish mother or one who has converted to Judaism according to *Halacha*. Conversion requires:

1. A fundamental commitment to all the laws and customs of Judaism, together with in-depth study of Torah so that one understands the rules and responsibilities

2. Ritual circumcision for men, even if previously circumcised

3. Immersion in a *mikvah*, ritual bath, for both men and women

4. Confirmation by a qualified Rabbinic court

Some sincere rabbis have tried to short-cut the process. However, no matter how sincere the convert or the rabbi is, the conversion process must be followed to have any validity. Those rabbis who say that we can ignore certain laws in Judaism are not qualified to convert anyone, because they don't believe or observe those laws of Judaism. To use an analogy: to become a citizen of the U.S., we must study about the country and agree to follow its regulations and responsibilities. We can't tell the judge, "I will only follow this law or not that one." At the same time, a judge who doesn't believe in the law isn't qualified to grant citizenship. Similarly, a convert can't refuse to keep certain *mitzvos as a pre-condition* to becoming Jewish, (e.g., *kashrus*, *Shabbos*, laws of *mikvah*, etc.). It doesn't make sense. Conversion to Judaism means adopting its obligations and responsibilities.

The bottom line is that Jews do not proselytize and generally discourage conversion. However, if a person is not just sincere, but is absolutely committed to living (and dying) as a Jew, then that person is welcomed as a member of the Nation of Israel. What's more, he or she can actually pray, "Blessed are You, L-rd, our G-d, G-d of our *forefathers, Abraham, Isaac, and Jacob.*"

Death (r'tz)

The Midrash offers the parable of two vessels, one leaving the harbor and the other entering it. As the one ship sailed out toward the open sea, all the people on the dock cheered and wished it well. Meanwhile, the crowd ignored the ship that pulled into the dock. A wise man addressed the people saying, "You are looking at things backwards. When a vessel leaves, you do not know what storms lay ahead or whether the ship will reach its destination. So there really is no reason to cheer. But when a vessel enters the harbor and arrives safely home, that is something to make you feel joy."

Life is that journey. When a child is born, we celebrate. When the soul returns home, we mourn. Yet if we viewed our existence on earth the way the wise man viewed the ship, perhaps we would have a different attitude. According to our sages, death is a temporary phenomenon. When *Moshiach* comes, G-d will remove the spirit of impurity from the earth and those who have passed on will live once again. So what is the purpose of death if we are all going to live again? Like an empty bucket that has been lowered into a river, the soul descends into this world void of *Torah* and *mitzvos*. When, after living a full and long life, the soul returns to its Maker, filled with *Torah* and *mitzvos*.

The Torah that the soul learned and the commandments it performed become "food" and "garments," enabling it to enjoy the splendor of G-d. If, for whatever reason, the soul did not live an observant Jewish life, it is still filled with thousands of hours of good thoughts, pleasant words, and kind acts, just as the bucket is full of water and fish. Through its positive acts in this world, the soul becomes "closer" to G-d than it was before descending to this level.

As Jews, we must realize that a person's life does not end with death. Nevertheless, we mourn and feel the loss in a very real way. In *Likutei Sichot, Volume 10,* the Lubavitcher Rebbe explains this apparent paradox:

> "The main connection between one person and another whom he loves is not a connection of the physical body (which is only flesh, sinew and bone), but one involving the qualities of the soul, which is the essential element of the person and indeed his essence.
>
> However, this connection between human beings is expressed by means of the body and its limbs, the eyes, ears, hands, power of speech, etc., in which and through which a person expresses his thoughts, emotions, and the particular characteristics of his soul, his essential element.
>
> It is therefore understood that neither the rifle's bullet nor the bomb fragment, the illness, or the like (although they may damage the body) can ever damage or detract from the soul. The death that is caused by the bullet or the sickness only separates the body from the soul, but the soul continues to live eternally, and continues its connection with those to whom it is closest. It grieves together with them in their sorrow and rejoices in their family celebrations. But the members of the family, living in this world, do not see this with their fleshly eye; they cannot touch it with their hands, as the physical connection has been broken."

Even though the physical bond between the soul and those who have remained "behind" has been broken, the spiritual bond can continue and even get stronger. We accomplish this by performing acts of kindness and goodness on behalf of the departed. For example, it is the custom for mourners to recite the *kaddish* prayer in the synagogue with a minyan. This prayer, interestingly, does not mention death. Instead, it serves to strengthen our relationship to G-d, which in turn, brings tremendous merit to the soul of the departed. If a person cannot recite *kaddish* for another, he or she can pay a worthy person (or institution) to make sure it is done. This cannot eliminate the responsibility of the mourner, yet it does enable to demonstrate his desire *that kaddish* be said. Besides saying *kaddish*, a person should give *tzedakah* in the merit of the soul. It is also a custom to learn *Mishnayos* (Oral Law) because the letters of the word *mishna* are the same as the word *neshoma* "soul." Another custom is establishing on-going activities in his or her name. These things help cleanse and elevate the soul to higher and higher levels of G-dliness. What's more, these things are especially important for a child to perform on behalf of a parent who has passed on. But what happens if the child is unable to learn or has no ability to give *tzedakah*? The answer is to live the most righteous life possible because, according to *Kabbalah* and *Chassidus*, every good thought, word or deed that a child performs is automatically "credited" to the parents, regardless of whether or not those activities were done specifically to benefit the parent. The reason is that the parents brought the child into the world, so they reap the rewards of the child's actions. (By the way, it makes no difference how old the "child" is. The parent remains a parent and, therefore, reaps the benefits of the good deeds done by the child.)

If a parent lost a child, G-d forbid, then the only way to benefit the child is to have him or her "in mind" when performing a *mitzvah* in thought, speech or deed. Similarly, if one wants to benefit another person, it is best to think of that person when performing a *mitzvah*.

Is it possible to mourn too much? Yes. The Torah dictates proper conduct, and an Orthodox rabbi can help answer any questions in this regard. The following two stories demonstrate the balance that we should strive to achieve.

Two Stories: One Lesson

Once there was a young scholar who practically lived in the Rebbe's Sholom Dov Ber's home. He forged a bond that we thought would be unbreakable. When the Rebbe passed away, the young scholar was inconsolable. We would often visit the Rebbe's resting place and beg, "Allow me to be with you." One night, the Rebbe appeared to his successor in a dream. He told the new Rebbe to inform the scholar to stop his emotional and irrational behavior. If he truly "loved" the Rebbe, he would follow the Rebbe's instructions and mode of conduct.

Crying doesn't accomplish anything. It "hurts" those above who are in a much higher and more enjoyable spiritual place, rather than giving them *nachas*.

In Crown Heights, NY, there lived a *chasid* who would open his doors to the entire neighborhood. One could not distinguish who was a friend, relative, or stranger. He continued this tradition for many years. The year after he passed away, his wife decided not to continue the tradition. Rather, she and her family would use the *sukkah* and then the lights would be turned off.

One way or another, the Lubavitcher Rebbe learned about the situation and sent the man's wife the following message: "How do you think your husband will feel when he visits his *sukkah* and finds that it is dark. If anything, you should make the celebration bigger than ever, so that it is clear that his spirit lives on." The widow took the Rebbe's advice and continued her husband's tradition.

One more thought: according to the Midrash, when G-d created life, He said *Tov.* "It is good." When He created death, He said *Tov M'od.* "It is very good." Why? As strange as it sounds, death defines life. If we never passed away, chances are, we would always postpone doing things. Understanding that our days are numbered gives us the drive to achieve. Not only that, once a person passes away, (G-d forbid), we can truly see and appreciate who he/she was (and continues to be on a spiritual plane.) We can see what the person has accomplished, recall the good deeds that are a part of us, and be grateful that we were allowed to walk this Earth together.

Nevertheless, we will not be whole until we are together again with our loved ones. For this reason, we pray daily for *Moshiach* and the Resurrection. May we immediately witness the day when G-d will wipe away all our tears by removing the spirit of impurity (death) from the world through *Moshiach*. Amen.

A True Kindness

The Torah established certain laws and customs to help us honor to the departed: They include the following:

Under Jewish law, the deceased may not be embalmed or cremated. Post-mortem examinations (autopsies) are forbidden, except where a reasonable likelihood exists that such an examination will contribute to saving the life of another patient at hand, or where an autopsy is required by civil law (*e.g.*, where death resulted from foul play). Competent Rabbinic authorities should *always* be consulted in the case of a "required" autopsy.

In addition, Burial should take place as soon as possible after death, and must include all body parts, as well as all materials containing the blood of the deceased (*e.g.*, clothes, bandages, sheets, etc.). Every Jewish community has a *Chevra Kadisha* ("Jewish Burial Society"). These G-d fearing Jewish men and women tend to the needs of the dead with the respect and sensitivity of one who cares for a baby. Their activities include "watching over" the body until burial (*Sh'mira*); physically cleansing the body; purifying it (*Tahara*); dressing the body in shrouds; and arranging for the burial (the *K'vurah*). This act is called a *Chesed Shel Emes*, a true kindness because the departed cannot "pay someone back." But you can be sure that G-d will.

The process of mourning starts immediately after the burial. To comfort mourners, it is traditional to say, "May you be comforted among the mourners for Zion and Jerusalem."

For Further Reading:

A View from Above
Rachel Noam
C.I.S. Publishers, 1993

The Jewish Mourner's Companion
Rabbi Zalman Goldstein
Jewish Learning Group, 2006

Toward a Meaningful Life,
Rabbi Simon Jacobson
William Morrow and Company, 2002

The Unheard Cry for Meaning
Viktor Frankl
Washington Square Press, 1997

18. Land of Israel

The Jewish people are connected by G-d to *Eretz Yisroel*, the Land of Israel. Rabbi Shlomo Yitzchaki (RASHI), the famous 11th century scholar, begins his commentary by quoting one of the Tanaim: "Rabbi Isaac said: The Torah which is the law-book of Israel should have begun with the verse, "This month shall be to you the first of the months," which is the first commandment given to Israel. What is the reason, then, that it begins with the account of creation: in order that He might give them the heritage of the nations. Should the nations of the world say to Israel, "You are robbers, because you took by force the lands of the seven nations of Canaan." Israel may reply to them, "All the earth belongs to the Holy One, blessed be He; He created it and gave it to whom He pleased. When He willed, He gave it to them, and when He willed, He took it from them and gave it to us."

Abraham received Israel as a heritage, as the Torah states (*Beraishis* 7:5-7) "And Abram took Sarai his wife, and Lot his brother's son and all their substance that they had acquired, and the souls that they had gotten in Haran; and they went forth to the land of Canaan and they came into the land of Canaan. And Abram passed through the land of Canaan to the place of Shechem, to Alon Moreh. And the Canaanite (tribe) was then in the land. And the Eternal appeared to Abram, and said, "Unto your seed will I give this land...."

G-d's pledge was formalized in the ceremony in which Abraham took four animals and divided them. (The four animals represented the four times the Jewish people would be exiled.) This ceremony, called the *Brit bein HaBesarim* ("Covenant between the Pieces") took place in 1743 BCE.

G-d re-established the right of the Jewish people to the land at Mount Sinai with the Giving of the Ten Commandments in the year1315 BCE. Forty years later, the Jewish people entered the land and began to conquer it. The Jews remained on the land for the next 3000 years. During that time, they settled Hebron and Schem (The Torah records the purchase of both areas.), Tiberias, Safed, Jerusalem, and dozens of other cities. The Jews built the First and Second Holy Temples. Even after the destruction of the Second Temple by the Romans in 70 CE, the Jews retained their connection to the land of Israel. Of the 613 commandments in the Torah, the majority are associated with the Land of Israel.

Our sages ask, "Why is the country called "*Eretz Yisroel,*" the *land* of Israel?" They answer, "Because the land "runs" to do the will of its Master." In Hebrew, the word for "land," *Eretz,* has the same root as *ratza,* "to run." It also shares the same root as *ratzon,* "will." The lesson is that G-d, in essence, "owns" the Land of

Israel. In fact the Torah (*Devorim* 11:12) testifies that Israel is "a land that the L-rd your G-d cares for; the eyes of the L-rd your G-d are always upon it from the beginning of the year to the end of the year."

G-d gave it to the Jews as long as they follow the laws of the Torah and perform *mitzvos.* If the Jews, G-d forbid, follow their own inclinations, then eventually, the land will cast the inhabitants out (G-d forbid.) However, if the Jews follow the ways and the will of G-d, the land will blossom. Throughout history, no other nation has been able to truly settle the land or make it blossom because no other nation has such a close and intrinsic relationship.

The ultimate expression of the relationship between the Jewish people, the Land of Israel, and the Holy One, blessed be He is found in *Bais HaMikdash,* the Holy Temple. It was the place where the Divine Presence was revealed on earth.

The First Holy Temple lasted 410 years and was destroyed by Nebuchadnezzar of Bavel in 586 BCE. The Temple was rebuilt 70 years later and lasted 420 years. The Romans destroyed this Second Holy Temple in 70 CE.

Many miracles were associated with the Holy Temple.

For example, the Ark containing the Ten Commandments resided in the Holy of Holies, a chamber 30 feet square. The Ark measured approximately 5 feet long by 3 feet wide. The distance from one side of the Ark to the wall of the chamber was 15 feet. The distance from the other side of the Ark to the other side of the chamber was also 15 feet. Even though the ark was a physical object located in the center of the Holy of Holies, it did not take up space. In addition to the Holy Ark not occupying space, our sages (Pirke Avos 5:5) state that:

- No woman ever miscarried from the smell of the meat of the holy sacrifices.
- No fly was ever seen in the slaughterhouse.
- No impurity ever disqualified the High Priest on Yom Kippur.
- Rain never extinguished the fire on the woodpile on the altar.
- The wind did not disperse the vertically rising column of smoke from the altar.
- No defect was found in the *omer*, two loaves offered on *Shavuos*, or the weekly Showbread.
- The people stood crowded together, yet when they prostrated themselves in prayer, they had ample space.
- No serpent or scorpion caused harm in Jerusalem.
- No one ever said, "There is no room for me to stay overnight in Jerusalem."

During the times of the Holy Temples, all males would journey to Jerusalem for *Pesach*, *Shavuot*, and *Succos*. They would offer sacrifices and participate in joyous celebrations. According to our sages, it was a time "to see and be seen (i.e., by G-d)."

Today, we no longer have the Holy Temple. But, our sages state, only the stones have been destroyed, the Divine Presence remains. For that reason, it is forbidden to visit the location where the Temple once stood. Instead, we can pray by the

Western wall which is not part of the Temple itself. Rather, it is an outer wall that surrounded the Temple.

If the Holy Temple was G-d's "home," how could He have allowed it to be destroyed? According to Jewish law, it is forbidden to tear down or destroy a synagogue. *Chassidus* explains that the same law applies to the Holy Temple. However, there is one exception to the law. One is permitted to tear it down to build a larger or more honorable structure in its place. The First and Second Temples were destroyed. But we are confident that we will witness their replacement: the Third and final Holy Temple in Jerusalem. May it be rebuilt speedily in our days.

Words of Wisdom

G-d examined all the nations of the generation of the wilderness and found only Israel worthy to receive the Torah. He examined all the mountains and found none as worthy as Mount Sinai to receive that precious gift. He examined all the cities and only Jerusalem was found worthy of the Holy Temple. He examined and evaluated all the lands but found none so fitting for the Jewish people as Eretz Yisroel (*Vayikra Rabbah* 13:2)

"If the nations of the world would have known the value the Temple had for them, they would have surrounded it with royal forces in order to protect it." (*Midrash Raba*)

Jerusalem, in the future, will become the capital of the world. (*Shemot Rabbah* 23:11)

The air of Eretz Yisroel makes one wise. (*Bava Basra* 158b)

For Further Reading:

From Time Immemorial
Joan Peters
J K A P Pubns; 2001

Eyes Upon the Land
Rabbis Eliyahu Touger and Uri Kaploun
Sichos in English, 2001

Myth and Facts. A guide to the Arab-Israel Conflict
Mitchell Bard
WWW.MitchellBard.com/books.html

19. Moshiach

The word *Moshiach* means "anointed." According to Maimonides
(Hilchos Melachim 11:1):

> King *Moshiach*, the son of David, will in the future rise to
> reestablish the kingdom of David, as in the days of old. He
> will rebuild the Holy Temple, gather in all the dispersed
> children if Israel, and will re-establish all the laws, including
> the sacrificial offerings and Sabbatical and Jubilee years as
> discussed in the Torah...."

> ....He will cause all the nations of the world to serve and
> worship the Holy One, blessed be He, as it is said, "For then I
> shall overturn to the nations a pure speech, with which they
> shall all call out to the Name of the L-rd, and serve Him as
> one unified group carries a load on their shoulders, shoulder
> to shoulder."

In other words, *Moshiach* will be a human, born to human
parents. He will be a Torah scholar and sage, someone who is

exalted in both intellect and holiness, yet someone who represents the ultimate in humility. *Moshaich* will maintain an intense and personal interest in each individual. Through his wisdom, his understanding and his knowledge, he will help us to maximize our talents and capabilities. Through this selflessness, he too, will rise in his relationship with G-d.

Moshiach will purify and elevate the world so that all mankind can recognize and accept G-d as the true Ruler and King of creation. As Maimonides states in the Laws of Kings (12:5), "In that Era, there will be neither famine nor war, neither envy nor competition, for good things will flow in abundance and all delights will be freely available as dust. The occupation of the entire world will be solely to know G-d. The Jews will therefore be great sages and know the hidden matters, and will attain an understanding of their Creator to the extent of mortal potential; as it is written, (Isaiah 11:9) "For the world will be filled with the knowledge of G-d as the waters cover the ocean bed.[56]"

This is the Jewish vision of the Messianic Era. During this era, sorrow and sadness, pain and confusion, want and desire will disappear. G-d will become the ultimate reality and we will devote ourselves to strengthening the relationship between G-d and this physical world.

At some point during this era, Jews who have passed on will be resurrected to once again live as souls in bodies. This time, however, they will be cured of any illness or defect, so they can

---

[56] Alperowitz, Rabbi Y. Y., I Believe., Lubavitch Foundation, U.K., 1993, P. 13

worship G-d with a complete heart and soul. According to many sages, righteous non-Jews will also be resurrected.

Starting in 5751 (1990), the Lubavitcher Rebbe, Rabbi M. M. Schneerson began quoting the *Midrash Yalkut Shemoni*, "The time of your redemption has arrived." In essence, the Rebbe was telling us that *Moshiach* may be revealed at any second. It is still true today. What's more, we can hasten the process of *Moshiach's* revelation by advancing in matters of Torah and *mitzvos*. Each *mitzvah* we do, each act we perform brings us one step closer to that time. Non-Jews, too, can help by performing deeds of goodness and kindness. Together, we can make the dream of a better world a true and lasting reality. May it happen now.

Words of Wisdom:

Moshiach represents the pinnacle of all hoped-for good. (Alsheikh)

"Hearken and hear Israel This is the time marked for the redemption by *Moshiach*. The sufferings befalling us are the birth-pangs of *Moshiach*. Israel will be redeemed through *teshuva*. Have no faith in the false prophets who assure you of glories and salvation after the War. Remember the word of G-d, "Cursed is the man who puts his trust in man, who places his reliance for help in mortals, and turns his heart from G-d" (Jeremiah 17:5) Return Israel unto the Eternal your G-d, prepare yourself and your family to go forth and receive *Moshiach*, whose coming is imminent. (Rabbi Joseph I. Schneerson, HaYom Yom)

For Further Reading:

The Days Of Moshiach
Rabbi Menachem Brod
Sichot in English, 1993

As a New Day Breaks
Rabbi Eliyahu Touger
Sichot in English, 1993

To Live and Live Again
Rabbi Nisson Dubov
Sichot in English, 2000

20. Looking at the World Through Jewish Eyes

According to our sages, we should serve G-d with joy. Interestingly, many people equate joy with "happiness," which is a feeling of energy and pleasure rolled into one. Hebrew and Yiddish don't have a word for "happiness." The word for joy, *simcha*, combines a feeling of attachment, love, purpose, hope, and optimism. It expresses the awareness that we are doing what we should—living according to the Will of G-d.

Simcha comes from knowing that G-d loves us and has given us the privilege of a) being aware of that love and b) being able to reciprocate that love by performing Torah and mitzvos. By associating our thoughts, words, and deeds with the commandments we strengthen our relationship with G-d, who is the source of all happiness and joy. What could be better?

The following story illustrates the concept:

Rabbi Mendel Futerfass was one of the spiritual advisors of Chabad. In the 1930's, he was sent to Soviet Prison for teaching children Torah. One time, he happened to share his jail cell with several prisoners. It was dark, damp, and cold. The food (what there was of it) barely kept them alive. No one knew what the next moment, much less the next day, could bring. Yet, despite the harsh conditions, Reb Mendel began singing a Chabad *niggun* (tune) to himself. His fellow prisoners were amazed.

"How can you be so happy?" one prisoner asked Reb Mendel.

"How can you be so sad?" Reb Mendel asked in return.

"I used to be a very influential lawyer. I had everything wealth, power, prestige. But I got caught in a political purge and now I've lost everything. I am ruined."

"The same here," Another prisoner spoke up. "I used to be one of the biggest doctors in the land. But I was unable to cure one person; and because of that, I was sent to prison. Now my career is over."

Both men looked at Reb Mendel, "And what about you?"

"I too have suffered. I was torn from my family and being for the "crime" of teaching little children. But despite it all, one thing hasn't changed: I was a servant of G-d before, and, no matter what the circumstances, I remain a servant of G-d now."

Every one of us is a servant of G-d. The key is to keep that in mind. Most of us live our lives from the "bottom up;" meaning that we focus on the here and now and pay little or no attention to our place in the grand scheme that links past, present and future. Trying to view things from the "top down" may help. G-d has a plan for the world and for every person in it. That plan encompasses past, present, and future. It involves our lives, as well as those of previous and future generations, and our part is infinitesimally small. Nevertheless, we are capable of handling every circumstance by maintaining our awareness of G-dliness and His constant involvement in our lives.

Another way to maintain the proper perspective is to bear in mind the Chassidic saying that, "A Chasid is a *tefach* (handsbreadth) above the world." In other words, we exist in the world, but we are neither confined nor brought down by it. Our souls are eternal and are continuously connected to the Eternal.

Obviously, it is easy to maintain a positive mental attitude as long as things are going relatively well. But what if they are not? What if our emotions are overwhelming our intellect? How are we supposed to get over it and get back on track? One way, is to look at adversity in this way:

Adversity.

Physics is Spirituality wrapped in the disguise of Nature.

Kites fly into the wind. So do gliders and planes.

But what has that got to do with me?

Because the very same wind that blows against airplanes

is *actually lifting them higher.*

So the next time the headwinds of life challenge you;

Remember, it's not the wind in your face that you feel,

But the lift beneath your wings helping you to soar.

Certainly viewing adversity as the wind beneath your wings can help a person cope. Here's another technique: Do not judge what you see for you are only seeing part of the picture.

For example, I once visited an old age home on Succos. I wanted to give the residents the opportunity to make a blessing over the lulav and esrog. I went into one resident's room. He was virtually unconscious, hovering between life and the opposite.

Based on his condition and the fact that he had been that way for weeks, I wondered whether he was accomplishing anything in this world at all. However, the Rabbi who was with me must have read my mind because he said, "He's here to give all those who take care of him that precious *mitzvah*." I went back and gently put his hands on the *lulav* and *esrog*, brought the two together, and whispered the blessing in his ear. I thought I was doing a *mitzvah* for him, but he was doing a *mitzvah*—for me.

There is another situation that you'll no doubt see again and again—something that at first glance appears to a curse, but then turns into a blessing. Adam Kellerman (www.adamkellerman.com) was a normal boy who loved athletics. Shortly before his bar mitzvah, he began to have pain in his hip and leg. The doctors found a tumor. Eventually won the war against his disease; however, it cost him the mobility of his leg. He was a boy who loved sports (especially hockey) and could no longer play them. Without going into the entire story, he was introduced to wheelchair tennis. Now, at the age of 22, he travels the world playing professional tennis—from his wheelchair. He has been to places, met people, and experienced the adrenalin rush of a professional sport that would have been beyond his wildest dreams. True, it happened through what could be considered a curse, but he made it into a blessing.

On the other hand, what appears to be a great blessing may turn into the greatest curse. Jack Whittaker would support that statement. On December 25, 2002, he won what at the time was the largest jackpot in the history of the multi-state Powerball Lottery: $315 million. Rather than collect the money over a period of time, he received a check for over $100 million in cash. At the time, it appeared as if he could fulfill his dreams. But those dreams quickly became a series of nightmares. Over the last eight years, he has been assaulted and robbed; his beloved granddaughter, Brandi, died of a drug overdose; he has been arrested several times, gone in and out of rehab for alcohol, lost virtually all of his money, and is still facing lawsuits over bounced checks from various casinos, and even worse, over the drug-related death of Brandi's boyfriend, which occurred in his home. He says that his life has been cursed—and no one would disagree with him. [57],[58]

On a slightly different level, the Zohar states that this world is an *alma d'shikra,* "world of lies." What we see is colored by what we think is reality. Many years ago, Charles Shulz illustrated a comic strip that defines the situation. In the first three panels, Linus is

---

[57] According to Chassidic humor, three things must affect someone. Money has to make a person crazy. If a rich person isn't crazy, that means he isn't rich enough. Whiskey has to make a person drunk. If a person has taken whiskey but isn't drunk, he obviously hasn't had enough. Chassidic philosophy has to purify a person's character traits. If a person has learned a lot of Chassidus, yet remains unchanged, he hasn't learned enough.
[58] http://www.washingtonpost.com/wp-dyn/articles/A36338-2005Jan25_3.html

strutting around holding a balloon. In the last panel, Charlie Brown comments, "Pride of ownership." Every physical thing we own or would like to own is as transitory as Linus' balloon.

Rabbi Nachman of Bratzlav, a grandson of the Baal Shem Tov, told the story of a man who ran through a crowd of people clutching a closed fist. Everyone ran after him wondering what he was hiding. One person thought that he was holding diamonds. Another person was sure that he was hiding gold. A third person thought it was pearls. Each person was positive. Yet when they finally caught up with the individual and forced him to open his hand, they saw that that it was empty. It is the same with our imagination. We believe that certain things have certain traits. But our belief is based on our desires, not on the way things really are. Not only that, if we obtained them, we would find that they too are "empty." The fancy car is uncomfortable and outrageously expensive to maintain. The gorgeous house is empty and cold. Money doesn't bring happiness, only more choices and issues that must be addressed.

"Bats."

A friend of mine once inherited a 17-room mansion. This mansion had carved oak paneling from the floor to the ceilings, a huge formal dining room, and fully stocked library with fireplaces. Needless to say, it was very impressive. One day, I asked my friend, "How do you like living there?

"It's terrible," he replied. "Every night after dinner, we have to go upstairs and spend the evening on the second floor." Before I could ask why, he explained. "Our house is full of bats," he replied. "They're hiding somewhere downstairs and when it gets dark, they come out and fly around the first floor. We've had one exterminator after another in here, but we can't get rid of them." The people who lived there were prisoners in their own home. Like we said, it's never ever as good as it looks.

Understanding that (a) we do not really know what good is and (b) the "good" things that we see are never as good as they look, can help us maintain the proper perspective.

Yet there is another way to put things in perspective. King Solomon asked the wise men throughout his kingdom for a technique that would provide comfort when he was sad, and would help ground him when he was inclined to feel overjoyed due to material success. One day, a craftsman brought a gold ring engraved with the Hebrew letters, *gimmel, zayin, yud.*

"What do these letters mean?" King Solomon asked.

The craftsman replied, "They are the initials of the Hebrew words, *Gam zeh yaavor.* This, too, will pass."

So it is. The both the bad times and the good times in life will pass. All we can do is make the best of each moment; for life is like a spinning wheel. Sometimes we're on top and sometimes the opposite. That's just the way life is, even for someone as wise and as great as King Solomon.

What if you are upset over an injustice? According to our sages, you should remember Pirke Avos 2:1, which proclaims, "Know what is above you – an Eye that sees, an Ear that hears, and all your deeds are recorded in a book." Nothing is ever forgotten. If someone appears to have "gotten away with something," it's not true. Whether in this life or the next, the person will get what he truly deserves.

Looking at it from another perspective, the Previous Lubavitcher Rebbe would quote his great grandfather, the Tzemach Tzedek, *Tract gut vet zein gut*, "Think good and it will be good." By thinking good, we are "asking" G-d to reveal the goodness that is inherently there, and to make it obviously "good" so that we can see and appreciate it. In other words, a Jew must have *emunah*. It is typically translated as "faith," but it really means "conviction." Our conviction must be that a) G-d is the very definition of goodness; therefore whatever G-d does is ultimately for the good and b) it is His definition of goodness applies, not ours. To that end, the word *emunah* is related to the word, *uman*, meaning "craftsman." This hints that we must work on our faith like a craftsman works on his skills. Faith begins where our knowledge ends. Therefore, the more Torah knowledge we have, the greater our faith in G-d.

Earlier, we mentioned that the search for meaning drives man. What greater meaning can there be in life than to attach ourselves to G-d. Think about it. Music, art, theater, books (including this one) are products of human beings. Therefore, they are, by nature, limited in what can communicate and in the length of their existence. When we attach ourselves to G-d, we lift ourselves above the clouds and confines of this world and attach ourselves to the One Who Is, Was, and Will Be forever. What's more, the achievement of attaching ourselves to G-d occurs whenever we follow the Torah. This is the gift of Judaism and the ultimate answer to the search for meaning.

As we mentioned earlier, the sages state, *"Do not desire the table of Kings because your table is greater than theirs."*

It sounds strange. Jewish sages are known for their insight. So how can the Shabbos table of the poorest and simplest Jew exceed the glory of a state dinner at Buckingham Palace or the White House? The answer depends upon your measuring system. While the table of kings can indeed be impressive, there is no place for children, no role for young adults, and only a minor ceremonial presence for elder statesmen. The table of kings is only focused on kings.

The Shabbos table of a Jew, and by extension Judaism, has a place and a role for everyone—children of all ages, young adults, parents, grandparents, relatives, and guests. Sitting at a *Shabbos* table means, families and friends share their lives as well as their traditions, experiences, and knowledge. They are part of a continuum that stretches from our forefather Abraham to *Moshiach* and beyond.

If a couple is fortunate enough to become observant when they are young enough to marry and raise a Jewish family in a traditional way, they experience milestones that shine like diamonds in one's life—circumcision, first haircut, bar or bas mitzvah, etc. Hopefully, their children will marry and have children, giving the couple the joy of becoming grandparents.

If a person, for whatever reason, didn't marry or raise a family, Jewish tradition allows that person to experience the stability, closeness, support and love of the community. Perhaps nothing illustrates this balance between the individual and community like the traditions of mourning. Typically, a Jew goes to a congregation for services every morning. But when a person is mourning, the congregation comes to him/her. They community visits him/her. The community supplies him/her with meals and fulfills any other requests. Wealth, power and status mean nothing. The poorest of the poor is treated the same as the richest of the rich.

A Jewish Mother

Many years ago, a Jewish mother passed away. She lived in poverty with her husband and three children. Baruch Hashem, she made sure to give her children a proper Jewish education and run her home according to tradition. She was a simple person and, to be honest, her presence wasn't felt by the movers and shakers of the Jewish community. But her passing was. The traditional Jewish community turned out for her funeral and a line of 40 to 50 cars followed the hearse.

Two ladies walked by the procession. "Wow. That person must have been wealthy." one woman said.

"Yeah." her friend agreed. "Look at that line of cars."

If only they knew the truth. She was wealthy—but in the kind of wealth that can't be measured here on Earth.

Words of Wisdom

"Don't think, do." Rebbetzin Shulamit Kazen

"What does G-d require of you but to do justly, to love mercy, and to walk humbly with your God." (*Micah* 6:8)

"It is a very near thing to you (to follow the Torah) in your mouth, in your heart, to do it." (i.e., in your thought, speech, and deed.) (*Devorim 30:14*)

21. The Next Step

Living a Jewish life (e.g., becoming *frum*, "observant") is *a process*, not a destination. Whether a person is born Jewish or converted, one proceeds on a path of spiritual growth, observing more and more. The key is to set times for learning, at least a little in the morning and a little in the evening. One should also learn *halacha l'maasa* practical laws, as well as those things that interest you, e.g. Jewish philosophy, mysticism, history, etc. No matter what you learn, success comes from concentration and from reviewing the material.

In general, learning is most effective when it's done out loud and with someone else. In fact, the classic style of study is *b'chavrusa*, with a study partner. The idea of study partners makes a lot of sense for many reasons. Having a partner can keep you from becoming too lazy to learn. A partner can help explain a concept. At the same time, when you explain something to your partner, you also help strengthen the learning experience for yourself.

In addition to a study partner, every person should have a *rabbi*, someone who can answer questions of Jewish law and practice.

Ideally, you should also have a *mashpia,* a spiritual advisor. This is a person who can help you grow spiritually. Your *rabbi* can be your *mashpia.* Your *mashpia* can also be someone who is older or more religious. Whoever you choose, he or she should be someone who is ready to listen and guide you along the path.

One final story: For several years, the rabbis of the Talmud debated the question, "What is the most important sentence in the Torah?" When the time came to render a decision, the first rabbi got up and stated that *Shema Yisroel Ado-noi Elo-heinu Ado-noi Echad,* "Hear O Israel, the L-rd is our G-d, the L-rd is One " is the most important sentence in the Torah because it crystallizes man's relationship to G-d. Another rabbi spoke. He believed that *V'ahavta Lireyecha Camocha,* "You should love your neighbor as yourself," is the most important sentence because it summarizes man's relationship to his fellow man. Finally, a third rabbi spoke. "In my opinion, *Es Hakeves Echad Taaseh Baboker v'Ais Hakeves Hasheini Taaseh Bain Haarbayim,* "You shall offer one lamb in the morning and the second lamb toward evening" is the most important sentence in the Torah. The rabbi's statement was met by jeers. The Holy Temple was destroyed. No one could offer sacrifices. How could this sentence capture the essence of Judaism? "Please let me explain," the rabbi began. "The entire purpose of the Torah is to do, to keep trying, day in and day out, morning and evening. Noble ideas and brilliant concepts are merely words in the wind without action. By commanding us to offer one lamb every morning and another lamb every evening, the Torah is teaching us that action is the key to accomplishment." Needless to say, the rabbis agreed.

We hope that this book will lead you to take those steps. May your journey be a pleasant and productive one, and may we meet on the streets of Jerusalem with *Moshiach*.

22. The 13 Pillars of Faith

The following 13 Principles of Faith are more than a list of important ideas. Formulated by Maimonides, they represent the very foundation of the Jewish way of life. No wonder that many people recite them every morning after *Shacharit* prayers.

I believe with complete faith

1. that the Creator, blessed be His Name, creates and guides all creatures, and that He alone made, makes, and will make everything.
2. that the Creator, blessed be His Name, is absolutely unique and that there is nothing else like Him and that He alone is our G-d, He alone always was, and He alone always will be.
3. that the Creator, blessed be His Name, is not a physical being, that nothing physical can ever affect Him, and there is nothing in the world which is comparable to Him.
4. that the Creator, blessed be His name, is the first and the last.
5. that to the Creator, blessed be His name, and to Him alone, it is proper to pray, and it is not proper to pray to anyone [or anything] else besides Him.
6. that the words of the prophets are true.

7. that the prophecy of Moses our teacher, may peace be upon him, was true, and that he was the father of all the prophets, those who came before him, and those who came after.

8. that the entire Torah now in our hands is the same Torah that was given to Moses our Teacher, may peace be upon him.

9. that this Torah will not be exchanged, nor will there ever be another Torah from the Creator, blessed be His Name.

10. that the Creator, blessed be His Name, knows all the deeds of men and all their thoughts, as it is said, "It is He Who fashions the heads of them all together; it is He who understands their deeds"

11. that the Creator, blessed be His Name, rewards those who keep His commandments.

12. in the coming of *Moshiach*, and even though he may delay, I still wait every day for him to come.

13. that those who died will be brought to life at whatever time it shall please the Creator, blessed be His Name and exalted is His remembrance forever and for all eternity.

Appendix I. Bridging the Unbridgeable

According to *Kabbalah* and *Chassidus*, G-dliness can express itself in two ways: The transcendent state is called, *Sovev Kol Almin*, meaning "G-dliness that encompasses all worlds." Viewed from the perspective of G-d's transcendence, the worlds are nothing, in much the same way that *rays* of sunlight do not exist within the sun.

The second way that G-dliness expresses itself is through what *Kabbalah* and *Chassidus* call, *Memale Kol Almin*. This refers to G-d's Immanence, the Divine Presence that "Fills the worlds" and keeps them existing.

Even though G-dliness is expressed through His Transcendence and Immanence, these manifestations could not create a physical world that totally conceals its Maker. To do that, G-d hid both the reality and revelation of his Being. This process is called *tzimtzum*, which means "Contraction." Keeping in mind the incomparability of Creator to creation, G-d "contracted" the revelation of His Existence to create five realms of G-dliness.

The highest world is called *Keser Elyon* or *Keser* "Crown." It is the G-dliness that exists after the first contraction yet before any type of revelation. *Keser* remains united with Divinity. *Keser* is composed of *Teinug* "Pleasure" and *Ratzon* "Will."

The next world down is *Atzilus* "the World of Emanation." In Hebrew, the word a*tzilus* means both "separation" and "near." On one hand, *Atzilus* represents a step removed from G-dliness. It is "separated" from its Divine Source. On the other hand, *Atzilus* does not "feel" separated at all. Rather it still reflects Divinity, i.e., it is still "one" with its Divine Source.

The next level down is *Beriah,* "the World of Creation." Here, G-dliness is so concealed that this level of existence "feels" independent. It cannot grasp the existence of *Atzilus*, the world that preceded it and allowed it to come into being, nor cannot it grasp the G-dliness that exists prior to *Atzilus*.

The next level down is *Yetzirah* "the World of "Formation". Again, this world is infinitely lower than *Beriah*, as well as *Atzilus* The next level down is *Asiyah* (the World of "Action."). It contains spiritual as well as material planes of existence. This physical world is the lowest of all. G-dliness is so concealed that created beings can actually deny the existence of our Creator.

In short, G-d "constricted" the revelation of His being so that creation could exist. This resulted in the levels of *Keser, Atzilus, Beriah, Yetzirah,* and last (as well as least), *Asiyah.* Each of these worlds has no conception of the world above it. *Kabbalah* and *Chassidus* call this state *Yesh MeAyin,* "Something from Nothing," where the "nothing" is the higher world and the "something" is the lower world that differs radically from it.

In *Yesh MeAyin*, the break appears to be absolute. Yet within each level, a different process takes place. It's called *Ilah v' olul,* "Cause and Effect." The process of cause and effect enables G-dliness to be revealed on lower and lower levels. Kaballah teaches that there are ten "levels." Each level is a Divine power and relates to existence in a very specific manner. The levels are *Chochma* "Wisdom,", *Bina* "Understanding," *Daas* "Knowledge," *Chesed* "Kindness," *Gevurah* "Severity/judgement," *Tiferes* "Beauty," *Netzach* "Victory," *Hod* "Splendor/Acknowledgment," *Yesod* "Foundation," and *Malchus* "Kingship."

Man, too, possesses 10 powers or faculties. Just as in G-dliness, these faculties descend in a relationship called the *Seder Hishtalshalus*, "Chain-like order of descent." In this configuration, the bottom rung of the ladder (i.e., stage of revelation) serves as the top rung of the latter that descends below it. We will describe this order, as expressed through man's 10 faculties, in Appendix II.

Appendix II. Souls and Soul Powers

As mentioned earlier, every person as a *Nefesh HaBahamis* "animal soul" and a *Nefesh HaSichlis* an "intellectualizing soul." Jews also have a spark of G-dliness called, the Nefesh Elokis.

The *Nefesh Elokis* has five descending levels that mirror the five-step downward progression of the spiritual worlds. The five descending levels from top down are *Yechida* "singular/oneness," *Chaya* "life force," *Neshoma* "breath," *Ruach* "spirit", *and Nefesh* "living soul". Rabbi Chaim Luzzatto[59], writing in *Derech Hashem* explains the relationship between the G-dly soul and the five levels this way:

> Even though this divine soul is often referred to as a single entity, it actually consists of a number of divisions on different levels. We can therefore say that there are actually a number of souls, bound together like links in a chain. Just as all these links comprise a single chain, so do all these levels of the soul constitute a single entity, which is called the divine soul. Each of these levels is bound to the one below it, until the lowest one is bound to the animal soul, which in turn is linked to the blood...[60].

---

[59] Rabbi Moshe Chaim Luzzatto (1707–1746), was a great Italian Rabbi and author of many classic works such as The *Path of the Righteous* and *The Way of G-d* (Derech Hashem).
[60] Luzzatto, Rabbi Moshe Chaim, *Derech Hashem*, translated by Aryeh Kaplan, Feldheim Publishers, New York, 1983, p. 179-181

The 10 Soul Powers

Each soul "contains" 10 soul powers[61]. The level prior to revelation is called *Keser* ("Crown") and contains two levels *Teinug* ("Pleasure") and *Ratzon* ("Will.") Out of that level, the first soul power to be revealed is called *Chochmah*, which means "Wisdom." It refers to the instantaneous flash that contains an idea or a concept. To put it another way, it is the spontaneous insight that suddenly grabs you, the "Eureka." moment. *Chochmah* contains the core of the idea and within that kernel, the potential for everything that follows. However in order to grow, it needs the nurturing capabilities of the next soul power, called *Bina*.

Bina means "Understanding." It is the feminine quality that nurtures the idea by identifying and integrating its qualities and characteristics. *Bina* enables the spark to become a flame. Without *Bina*, the spark would return to the hidden world that initiated it. For example, if you don't concentrate on a sudden idea, it's lost.

Combining *Chochma* and *Bina* results in *Daas*. It means "Knowledge that comes from unification," i.e., focusing on a concept until it becomes known. In the Bible (Genesis, 4:6), we find that "Adam knew Eve." The Hebrew word used is *yada*, a form of the word *Daas*. In this context, the phrase would mean "Adam bound himself to Eve."

---

[61] This reflects the composition of the five worlds (*Keser, Atzilut*, etc.) which each contain 10 levels.

Chochmah, *Bina*, and *Daas* are building blocks the same way that proteins are the building blocks of DNA. Just like the union of Adam and Eve led to the births of Cain and Abel, the union of *Chochmah* and *Bina* through *Daas*, "gives birth" to emotional attributes. The first is *Chesed*, translated as "Kindness."

Chesed is the power to give without restrictions or limits. On the positive side, it serves as the force behind all activity. It also allows disparate attributes/powers to connect with each other. On the negative side, too much *Chesed* can be destructive. For example, parents naturally love their children and want to make them happy. But too much *Chesed* could spoil them, and result in destructive behavior.

That's where the soul power of *Gevurah* comes in. It manifests itself as "Severity/Judgment," and other similar traits. In essence, it is the strength to set limits. Obviously, just as too much *Chesed* is not productive, too much *Gevurah* is also not productive.

The third soul power is called *Tiferes* "Beauty." It balances *Chesed* and *Gevurah*, and serves as the source of harmony. *Tiferes* is sometimes known by another term, *Rachamim*, which means "compassion." Compassion synthesizes love and restraint. While it searches for a compromise between these two attributes, it typically emphasizes the power of love.

How does *Rachamim* differ from *Chesed*? Suppose asks you for a job; if you give it to him, you have performed an act of *Rachamim*. If he does not deserve the job but you offer it, you have just performed an act of *Chesed*.

We began by stating that the intellectual faculties of *Chochma*, *Bina* and *Daas* can give birth to emotional attributes of *Chesed*, *Gevurah*, and *Tiferes*. These attributes can, in turn, give birth to the next three, *Netzach*, *Hod* and *Yesod*.

Netzach means "Victory." It is the ability to overcome all obstacles, to the point of not even recognizing them, in order to fulfill one's desire. *Netzach* also expresses itself as "Eternity," which, in essence, represents the ultimate state of victory.

Hod includes "Splendor/Acknowledgement." *Hod* complements the power of *Netzach* by subordinating oneself to a higher authority to the point of self-sacrifice. *Hod* also means "glory," which is the revelation of a higher power to those who deserve it.

Yesod represents "Foundation," i.e., the link that is established between the giver and the recipient. Just as the foundation connects the building to the ground, so *Yesod* connects the one who gives to the one who receives. In this context, *Yesod* channels all the previous faculties toward achieving a specific end.

To summarize, the desires and yearnings of one's soul develop and become revealed through *Chochma*, *Bina*, and *Daas*. These yearnings evolve through *Chesed, Gevurah, Tiferes*, and further develop through *Netzach, Hod*, and *Yesod*. At this point, they have reached the brink of actuality.

The final soul power or attribute is called *Malchus* or Kingship. *Malchus* is compared to speech (e.g., the mouth) that reveals hidden thoughts and ideas. Both the mouth and the faculty of speech are merely vessels, expressing what the mind that wishes to communicate. So too, *Malchus* is the vessel that reveals what was previously hidden to a recipient.

Each attribute contains and is influenced by the other nine. In *Chochmah*, you have *Bina*, *Daas*, etc. Within *Bina*, you have *Chochmah*, etc. Like spiritual DNA, these powers combine in many ways to accommodate the amazing variety of created beings, both terrestrial and supernal.

In a deep Chassidic discourse, Rabbi Joseph I. Schneerson[62], the Previous Lubavitcher Rebbe, describes how the 10 attributes of the G-dly soul can help connect man to his Divine source:

> Jews refine and elevate the world by utilizing the G-dly intellectual and emotive traits of their divine soul. *Chesed* is the natural and instinctive love possessed by the G-dly soul for G-d. *Chesed* within *Chesed* is the revelation of this natural love, that it be revealed within all his powers and not limited only to the heart....*Gevurah* within *Chesed* is enmity to those who hate G-d, as the verse states: Those who love G-d, despise evil.." (Psalms 97:10) ....*Tiferes* within *Chesed* is utilizing all one's inner beauty for (the adornment and splendor of) Torah and *mitzvos*, (as the verse states,) "And his heart was lifted up in the ways of the L-rd."....[63]

However, the vitalizing animal soul is also composed of these 10 attributes. Controlled, they can be used in a positive manner.

[62] Rabbi Joseph Isaac Schneerson, (1880-1950) who fearlessly fought to preserve traditional Judiasm under the Bolshevik and Communist regimes in Russia.
[63] Schneerson, Joseph Isaac, *Chassidic Discourses*, Kehot Publication Society, NY, 1986, Pages 210-211

Unchecked, they can bring man down below the level of an animal, as the Rebbe relates:

> *Chesed* [of the animal soul and selfish inclination] is love of material and corporeal matters. *Chesed* within *Chesed* is the enthusiasm and delight, may Heaven protect us, derived from gross physical and material matters and worldly suppositions. *Gevurah* within *Chesed* of the animal soul is the ambivalence or even enmity felt toward one who observes Torah and *mitzvos*. *Tiferes* within *Chesed* is [expressed when] "For the wicked boasts of his heart's desire..." (Psalms 10:3)...[64]

The Power of the Soul

The following event may put one's soul powers into a more recognizable context. Many years ago, George M., went on his honeymoon. What should have been a carefree time became a nightmare when his wife (a nurse) discovered a growth on his arm. The biopsy confirmed their fears. He immediately began receiving chemotherapy and radiation, but the treatments did not work. The doctors waited for him to recuperate, then offered him a choice. He could go for another round of chemo or he could go home. George decided to go home.

Several weeks before he died, George's buddies decided to take him to a Boston Celtics basketball game. He was too weak to walk by himself, so they had to help him into the car. His wife promised to watch the game on TV, hoping to get a glimpse of him having a good time with his friends. It was a hard-fought

---

[64] Ibid, p. 212

game and toward the end, one of the Celtics scored a key basket. The crowd went wild and the TV cameras turned toward the stands. As his wife watched in astonishment, George jumped to his feet, pumping his arms up and down in victory. When he returned home that evening, George was so physically and emotionally exhausted that his buddies had to carry him into the house. But for that one brief moment, the old George was back.

What George's wife saw, and what can be seen in any sports event, is an open expression of *netzach*—the drive to victory. Everyone has it to some extent. Under the right circumstances, however, it can make the body do incredible things.

Appendix III. The Chain of Scholarship

Let's follow that chain of scholarship from the Torah, through the *Mishna*, *Gemara*, *Rishonim* (early Rabbis such as Maimonides), and *Acharonim* (later Rabbis) until the development of the Code of Jewish Law, as it applies to the prayer *Shema*.

The Torah (Devorim Chapter 6, Verses 4 – 7) states:

1. *"Hear (i.e., Comprehend) O Israel, The L-rd our G-d, the L-rd is one.*

2. *And you shall love the L-rd your G-d with all of your heart, and with all of your soul, and with all of your might.*

3. *And these words (shall be) that I command you this day, shall be upon your heart.*

4. *And You shall teach them diligently to your children, and you shall discuss them when you sit in your house, when you walking along the way, and when you lie down and when you rise up."*

According to these verses, we have a commandment to say "*these words*" at specific times. But the verses do not define what "*these words*" are, or "*when you lie down and when you rise up.*"

The Mishnah States

The *Mishna* records the Oral Law that was given to Moses along with the written Torah. It begins to add flesh to the bare bones of the commandment. The Mishna was written in a very concise form. For example, *Mishna Berachos* begins:

1:1 From what time are we to read *Shema* in the evening? From the moment when the priests enter (their home) to eat of their priest's due, up until the end of the first watch. This is the opinion of Rabbi Eliezer, but the Sages say, 'Until midnight.' Rabban Gamaliel says, 'Until dawn."

It happened once that his sons returned from a festive meal and said to him, "We have not yet read the *Shema*.' He told them, 'If dawn has not yet appeared, it is your duty to recite it.' And not only in this case, but in all cases whether the Sages say, 'Until midnight,' the obligation may be carried out until dawn; for example, burning fat and limbs (on the altar in the Holy Temple) may be performed until dawn, and all the (sacrifices) must be eaten on the same day have their proper times until dawn. If so, why say, 'Until midnight?' to keep man from transgressing.

1:2 What time does one begin to recite *Shema* in the morning? When one can discern between the colors blue and white. Rabbi Eliezer says, 'Between blue and green (and concludes by sunrise. Rabbi Joshua says, 'Until the third hour, because it is the habit of kings to rise at the end of the third hour. He who reads (*Shema*) later has not lost thereby, for it is as one who reads in the Torah.

1:3 The School of Shammai maintains, in the evening one should lie down and recite (*Shema*) and in the morning one should stand up, because the verse says, "And when you lie down and when you rise up." But the School of Hillel maintains that everyone should read it in the position he happens to be, as the verse says, "and when you walk along the way." If so, why does it say, "And when you lie down and when you rise up? (The School of Hillel maintains it means, "At the time when people lie down and at the time when people get up.")

The Talmud States

The *Talmud Berachos* explains the statements found in the *Mishna*. It dedicates 20 folios (front and back pages) to this *mitzvah* and the sages' comments. The *Talmud Berachos* begins:

"What (source) does the Tanna (rabbi) use for starting (the Mishna with the words), "From what time?"

Further, why does he deal first with the evening *Shema*? Let him begin with the morning *Shema*.

(The Gemara answers) The Tanna bases himself on the Torah, "when you lie down and when you rise up."

The *Talmud* continues recording the free flow of conversation as the Rabbis try to understand the Torah and *Mishna*. Throughout the ages, rabbis wrote seforim that distilled the law from the language in the Talmud.[65]

The Rabbis State

Between the years 1170 and 1180 Common Era, Rabbi Moshe ben Maimon (Maimonides also known as the Rambam) completed, the *Mishneh Torah,* one of the most comprehensive collections of

---

[65] In general, three classic periods of scholarship helped to codify and lay the foundation for the laws that we follow today-- the Geonim 6th – 10th centuries CE); the Rishonim 11th – 15th centuries CE; and Acharonim, 16th – 18th centuries CE.

Jewish Law published. It included laws that were relevant to Jewish living outside the land of Israel, as well as laws that pertained to Jews living during the times of the Holy Temples. On the topic of Shema, Maimonides writes:

1:1 We are obligated to recite the *Shema* twice daily – in the evening and in the morning, as the verse states: '...when you lie down and when you rise...' i.e., when people are accustomed to sleep, this being the night, and when people are accustomed to rise, this being daytime.

1:2 What does one recite? These three sections:

"Hear O Israel" (*Devorim* 6:4-9)

"And if you will listen" (*Devorim* 11:13-21) and

"And G-d said.." (*Bamidbar* 15:37-41)

We begin with the section of "Hear O Israel" since it contains the unity of G-d, the (commandment) to love Him, and to study Torah; since it (Torah study) is the foundation upon which everything is based. After, (we read), "And if you will listen..." since it contains the command to fulfill the rest of the *mitzvos*; and finally, (we read) the portion of *tzitsis* (ritual fringes) since it also contains the command to remember all the *mitzvos*.

1:3 The commandment of *tzitsis* is not obligatory at night. Nevertheless, we recite the Torah section that describes *tzitsis* because we are commanded to mention the Exodus from Egypt both during the day and at night as *Devorim* 16:3 says, "In order that you remember the day of your leaving the land of Egypt all the days of your life."

Maimonides continues to discuss what blessings are said before *Shema* and what blessings are said after, what happens if one read it before the proper time, or after the proper time, what is the proper language to use for reciting *Shema*, and many other topics related to this prayer. In all, Maimonides' Laws of the *Shema* contains four chapters and 57 detailed laws.

Maimonides' *Mishneh Torah* remains one of the greatest works of scholarship in Jewish history. However, Maimonides did not provide the sources he used to base his decisions. In addition, other great Rabbis differed with Maimonides on the law as it was to be followed. Some five hundred years later, Rabbi Yosef Caro (1488–1575) authored the *Shulchan Aruch* ("Prepared table"). It dealt only with the laws applicable during the period of the Diaspora and was written in a brief, almost terse style. The *Shulchan Aruch,* like the *Mishneh Torah*, was designed so that the laws could now be applied by anyone who could read and understand simple Hebrew. Arranged and codified the laws according to the customs and traditions of the Sephardic Jews of the time, it has become the standard reference for Jewish law. Rabbi Moshe Isserles (1525–1572) added the customs and traditions of the Ashkenazic Jewish tradition. However, the rabbis of each era afterward built upon that foundation.

Many divergent opinions about both laws and customs arose subsequent to the *Shulchan Aruch*, resulting in some confusion for the layman. To remedy this, in the mid-nineteenth century,

Rabbi Shlomo Ganzfried (1804–1886) authored the *Kitzur Shulchan Aruch*. It consolidated the laws that applied to daily life so that the average person or that era could use it as a reference. The section dealing with reciting *Shema* has one chapter and eight laws. This is how Rabbi Ganzfried introduces the obligation to recite the *Shema*:

> 1. The beginning of the time to recite the *Shema* is the same as earliest time one may put on *Tefillin*. The time for its recitation extends until the passage of one fourth of the day. In this context, a day is considered as lasting from dawn until the appearance of the stars at night. The most preferable way of fulfilling this *mitzvah* is to recite it when the pious would. They would prepare to recite the *Shema* shortly before the appearance of the sun so that they could complete the recitation of the *Shema* and its blessings together with the appearance of the sun, and immediately proceed to recite the *Shemona Esrai*. Whoever follows this practice will receive great reward....

> 2. The *Shema* may be recited whether sitting or standing. If one was sitting, it is forbidden to rise specifically in order to recite the Shema while standing. It is forbidden to recite the *Shema* while lying down. A person who is already lying down should turn to the side slightly and recite the *Shema*[66].

Rabbi Ganzfried continues describing the laws in the chapter.

---

[66] Ganzfried, Rabbi Shlomo, *Kitzur Shulchon Oruch*, translated by Rabbi Eliyahu Touger, Moznaim Publishing Corp., New York, 1991, P. 75

In addition to the *Shulchan Aruch* and other similar works, Jews throughout the centuries asked their Rabbis *she'eilos* "questions" on specific issues. Often, the Rabbis published their *teshuvos,* "answers," which other Rabbis cited when dealing with questions. For example, the following question was submitted to Rabbi Shmuel Abuhab (1610 – 1694). His response was published in his book, *Teshuvos Dvar Shmuel*:

> Q: Ten Jews, none of whom knows Hebrew live in a community where there is no one who can recite the prayers for them in Hebrew. Are they permitted to pray together and recite *Kaddish* and *Kedusha* (communal response in the *Shemoneh Esrai* prayer) in their own language?

> A: Although it may sound strange, most *poskim* (Jewish legal authorities) permit praying in any language. Proof of this is the *Kaddish* prayer, which is recited in Aramaic, and most *poskim* hold that Aramaic is inferior to any other language. An additional proof can be inferred from the verse, "Speak to Aharon and so his sons, saying: 'This is how you must bless the Israelites.' The implication is that the priestly blessing must be recited in Hebrew. It follows that were it not for this special injunction, even the priestly blessing could have been said in any language, just as can the *Shema*, the *Shemona Esrei* (prayer of 18 Benedictions), and *Birkas HaMazon* (Grace after Meals.)

Over the last 33 centuries, thousands of *she'eilos* and *teshuvos* have been written on all aspects of the Torah. If you have a question, ask your local Orthodox rabbi. Chances are, the question (or a variation) and the answer have been recorded in one of his books

Lists and Information

Tanach - The Twenty-Four Books of the Bible

The twenty-four books of the Bible are called the *Torah shebiksav* - the Written Law. The order presented here is the order in the Talmud (Bava Basra14b)

The Torah (The Five Books of Moses):

1. Bereishis (Genesis)

2. Shemos (Exodus)

3. Vayikra (Leviticus)

4. Bamidbar (Numbers)

5. Devorim (Deuteronomy)

Neviim (Prophets):

6. Yehoshua

7. Shoftim

8. Shmuel (Alef and Beis)

9. Melachim (Alef and Bais)

10. Yirmiyahu

11. Yechezkel

12. Yishayahu

13. Trey Assar (the Twelve Prophets)

Hoshea	Yona	Tzefanya
Yoel	Micha	Chaggai
Amo	Nachum	Zecharya
Chavakuk	Malachi	

Kesuvim (The Writings)

14. Ruth

15. Tehillim (Psalms)

16. Iyov (Job)

17. Mishley (Proverbs)

18. Koheles (Ecclesiastes)

19. Shir Hashirim (Songs of Songs)

20. Eicha (Lamentations)

21. Daniel

22. Esther

23. Ezra/Nechemya

24. Divrey Hayamim (Chronicles)

Chumash and Parshiyot

Bereishis (Genesis)

Bereishis

Noach

Lech Lecha

Vayera

Chayey Sarah

Toldos

Vayeytzey

Vayishlach

Vayeyshev

Mikeytz

Vayigash

Vayechi

Shemos (Exodus)

Shemos

Va'eyra

Bo

Beshalach

Yisro

Mishpatim

Teruma

Tetzaveh

Ki Sisaw

Vayakhel

Pekuday

Vayikra (Leviticus)

Vayikra

Tzav

Shemini

Tazriya

Metzorah

Achrey Mos

Kedoshim

Emor

Behar

Bechukosai

Bamidbar (Numbers)

Bamidbar

Naso

Beha'aloscha

Shelach

Korach

Chukas

Balak

Pinchas

Mattos

Mas'ai

Devorim (Deuteronomy)

Devorim

Ve'eschanan

Eykev

R'ay

Shoftim

Ki Seytzey

Ki Savoh

Nitzavim

Vayelech

Ha'azinu

Vezos Habrachah

39 Categories of Creative Activity Forbidden on Shabbos

The following activities were associated with building the Tabernacle in the desert. Since the Torah puts the commandment to cease work on *Shabbos* next to detailed instructions for building the *Mishkan*, the rabbis understood that these activities must be forbidden.

In general, these all demonstrate man's creativity or mastery over his environment. By forbidding these general categories of creative activity (as well as all subcategories and associated labors), the Torah reminds man (at least one day a week) that he is only a guest in this world, and not the owner. The laws of *Shabbos* are extremely complex. No assumptions should be made about what is, or is not considered creative activity without consulting a qualified rabbi.

1. Sowing: anything that encourages growth of plants

2. Plowing: improving soil for agricultural purposes

3. Harvesting: removing produce from its source of sustenance or place of growth

4. Making sheaves: gathering agricultural produce from its place of growth

5. Threshing: extracting of "food" from its "husk"

6. Winnowing: separating of "food" from its "husks" using wind

7. Selecting: removing "waste" from "food"

8. Grinding: making large particles into small particles by grinding or chopping

9. Sifting: separating fine and coarse particles using a sieve

10. Kneading: combining solid particles into one mass using a liquid

11. Baking: using heat to effect a change of state

12. Shearing: removal of fur or hair from a live animal

13. Washing: laundering or cleaning of absorbent materials

14. Combing: separating tangled fibers

15. Dyeing: permanently coloring materials

16. Spinning: twisting individual fibers into one thread

17. Setting up the loom

18. Threading the loom

19. Weaving: weaving of fibers, or basket-weaving, knitting etc.

20. Unraveling woven threads

21. Tying: tying a permanent or an artisan's knot

22. Untying: untying any of the aforementioned knots

23. Sewing: permanent bonding of two materials

24. Tearing: tearing permanently bonded materials for a constructive purpose

25. Hunting: capturing or trapping animals

26. Slaughtering: killing or wounding a living creature

27. Flaying: stripping the skin from a carcass

28. Salting: preserving or hardening of a substance using salt or chemicals

29. Tanning: softening and preparing leather

30. Scraping: smoothing a surface by scraping

31. Cutting: cutting materials to a specific size or shape

32. Writing: writing, drawing or marking

33. Erasing in order to write

34. Building: constructing dwellings or making implements

35. Demolishing in order to build

36. Extinguishing: putting out or diminishing a fire

37. Burning: igniting or increasing a fire

38. Finishing touches: completing or touching-up an object

39. Carrying: carrying from a private to a public domain and vice versa, or carrying in the public domain (Mishnah, Tractate Shabbos 7:2)

This list was taken from the book, *After the Return* by Rabbi Mordechai Becher's and Rabbi Moshe Newman, (Feldheim Publishing, 1995). It appeared on the Ohr Samayach web site: http://www.ohr.org.il/Shabbat/whatis.htm

Hebrew Letters and Words

Aleph - Beis: The Alphabet, Vowels, and Values

HEI (5)	DALET (4)	GIMMEL (3)	VEIS (2)	BEIS (2)	ALEF (1)
KAF (20)	YUD (10)	TES (9)	CHES (8)	ZAYIN (7)	VAV (6)
NUN (50)	FINAL MEM (40)	MEM (40)	LAMED (30)	FINAL CHAF (20)	CHAF (20)
FINAL FEI (80)	FEI (80)	PEI (80)	AYIN (70)	SAMECH (60)	FINAL NUN (50)
SIN (300)	SHIN (300)	REISH (200)	KUF (100)	FINAL TZADDIK (90)	TZADDIK (90)
		SAV (400)	TAV (400)		

Vowels (Nekudos)　　Sound Example

Patach	ahhh	father
Kamatz	aw	awesome
Cholam	oh	grow
Segol	eh	bed
Sh'va	stop or shortened sound	
Tzeirei	ay	play
Shuruk	oo	food
Kubutz	oo	food
Chirik	ee	feet

Numerals

Number	Masculine Form	Feminine Form
One	Echod	Achas
Two	Shenayim	Shetayim
Three	Shelosha	Shalosh
Four	Araba'a	Arba
Five	Chamisha	Chamesh
Six	Shisha	Shesh
Seven	Shiv'a	Sheva
Eight	Shemona	Shimoneh
Nine	Tish'a	Teysha
Ten	Asar'a	Eser
Eleven	Achad Asar	Achas Esrey
Twelve	Shneym Aser	Shteym Esrei
Thirteen	Shelosha Asar	Shelosh Esrei
Forteen	Arba'a Asar	Arba Esrei
Fifteen	Chamisha Asar	Chamesh Esrei
Sixteen	Shisha Asar	Shesh Esrei

Seventeen	Shiv'a Asar	Shevah Esrei
Eighteen	Shemonah Asar	Shemonei Esrei
Nineteen	Tisha Asar	Tisha Esrei
Twenty	Esrim	Esrim
Thirty	Shloshim	Shloshim
Forty	Arbayim	Arbayim
Fifty	Chamishim	Chamishim
Sixty	Shishim	Shishim
Seventy	Shvi'im	Shvi'im
Eighty	Shmonim	Shmonim
Ninety	Tish'im	Tish'im
Hundred	Meah	Meah
One Thousand	Elef	Elef

Web Resources

www.chabad.org – one of the most popular Jewish resources on the Internet

www.moshiach.com – Information on the Redemption

www.moshiach101.com – Information on Moshiach

http://www.torahcafe.com/ – On-line Torah classes

http://www.AscentOfSafed.com/ – on-line site for learning and living Chassidus and Kabbala

www.Luach.com – Jewish classified ads by region

http://www.jewishaudio.org – Jewish audio classes

http://www.thirtysix.org/ - Contemporary Jewish thought

www.inner.org - Kabballa from Rabbi Yitzchak Ginsburg

http://www.thereisone.com/ - Spirituality Gutman Locks

www.TheYeshiva.net – Classes by Rabbi YY Jacobson

http://halachafortoday.com/default.aspx - Jewish website features two Jewish laws per day

http://www.torahfax.net/ - dailyTorah thought

www.Judaism.com – On-line Jewish bookstore

http://www.hebcal.com/ – Hebrew-English Date Convertor

http://www.portraitofaleader.blogspot.com

http://www.israelnationalnews.com/ – Jewish news

http://www.jnet.org/ – On-line learning

19766016R00172

Made in the USA
Charleston, SC
10 June 2013